The
Slow-Release
Miracle

A Spirituality for a Lifetime

Andrew Nugent, OSB

Cover design by Trudi Gershenov
Book design by Lynn Else

Library of Congress Cataloging-in-Publication Data

Nugent, Andrew.
    The slow-release miracle : a spirituality for a lifetime / Andrew Nugent.
      p. cm.
    Includes bibliographical references (p.   ).
    ISBN 0-8091-4397-6 (alk. paper)
    1. Spiritual life—Christianity. I. Title.
    BV4501.3.N84 2006
    248.4′82—dc22

                                         2006001228

Published by Paulist Press
997 Macarthur Boulevard
Mahwah, New Jersey, 07430

www.paulistpress.com

Printed and bound
United States of A

Contents

CONTENTS

Acknowledgments

The following texts in translation are most generally used in this book:

For the Rule of Saint Benedict: *RB 1980: The Rule of St. Benedict in English,* ed. Timothy Fry, OSB, and others (Collegeville, MN: Liturgical Press, 1982)

For the works of John Cassian: *The Conferences* (1997) and *The Institutes* (2000), trans. Boniface Ramsey, OP (New York and Mahwah, NJ: Newman Press)

I am grateful to the respective translators, editors, and publishers for permission to use these texts.

To the monks of St. Benedict's Monastery,
Ewu-Ishan, Nigeria.
*"Wherever we may be, we are united in the service
of the same Lord"* (RB 61:10).

Introduction

Spiritual growth is always slow, in the sense that it takes as long as we have got: a whole lifetime, be that life long or short. It is what human life is all about.

Spiritual living is not a technique that can be picked up by basic training or learned from books. It is the manifestation of the Spirit. "These things will the Lord deign to show forth, through his Holy Spirit, in his workman now cleansed from vices and sins" (RB 7:70).[1] Saint Benedict's intuition is profoundly scriptural. Saint Paul writes, "We are what God has made us, created in Christ Jesus for good works, which he has prepared beforehand to be our way of life" (Eph 2:10). Even for God, a work of art, which is a work of love, cannot be rushed.

These are hard sayings for the proactive, for hands-on achievers, people who do it *their way* and expect results in a hurry. Such people are often dissatisfied with the Holy Spirit. Reading this book will not allay their disappointment. There will be no measurable results for their trouble—such as improved morals, progress in prayer, inner peace, being in control, or the quiet satisfaction of seeing oneself getting bigger and better every day and in every way.

A second disappointment, endemic to the spiritual life, is the discovery that, though this spiritual saga is indeed about ourselves, none of us gets to be center stage in our own story. The initiative in that tragicomedy does not lie with our willpower, our intelligence, or our strength of character; it lies with a creative God who has brought us out of nothingness and who is still fashioning us into the fullness of life. This is what grace means: God's creative and highly inventive love working itself out in our becoming. "I waited patiently for the Lord," the psalmist sings (Ps 40:1). It is a good description of the spiritual life. Saint Benedict seems to understand how hard this waiting is for our pride and self-importance when he writes that it is by *patience* that we share in the sufferings of Christ (Prol. 50).

Which is not to say that this is a book in praise of hand-folding passivity. It is not. It is a book about a spiritual art of living. This art involves learning how to listen, how to trust, how to hope, and how to accept love. It is on that basis that we can begin to love in return, to live, and to act dynamically.

This is not so much a question of chronological sequence. Who could fail to appreciate the innocence and spontaneous generosity of children? But we do not remain children. The attractive goodness of childhood becomes denatured and artificial, regressive, or even calculating and manipulative if it is allowed to become a frozen mask of spontaneity and charm. One has only to think of those child actors who choose or are persuaded to stay cute for the sake of adult delectation, like latter-day *castrati*. Voices break and mature. The same is true of the spiritual life. There is a certain breaking, and a necessary deepening.

Morally and spiritually, the growing young person learns that being cute is no longer enough. An exodus and a journey become necessary. And so it is that, between the innocence of childhood and the spiritual integration of mature adult life—which in our culture is increasingly delayed into the late twenties or even into early middle-age—there lies a period of transition that can be both difficult and dangerous. This is the time when we realize the deep dividedness within ourselves, the struggle between good and evil, and our radical incapacity to create ourselves as good and loving persons. After the adolescence of the body and of the emotions, this is the adolescence of the soul, a time enlivened, indeed ennobled by desire, and as often disfigured by the spiritual acne of selfishness in all its hydra-headed forms.

A person may achieve a provisional equilibrium at this time in terms of professional, business, cultural, political, or even sporting projects and achievements, or in camaraderie, in sometimes very intense personal relationships, or simply in frenetic and obsessive absorption in entertainments and distractions of every kind. All of these experiences, even the best of them, are potentially forms of that escapism that consists in using good things foolishly and turning means into ends.

The first part of this book, "Points of Departure," is written for people like myself, who are spiritual adolescents. It tries to say how we need to grow up and get serious, how we need to tell ourselves and perhaps others the truth about ourselves, and to acknowledge that truth before God with humility and hope. Saint Antony of Egypt said, and many of the desert fathers loved to repeat after him, "Each morning I say to myself, 'Today, I will begin.'" This realistic and yet ever-hopeful attitude is indeed the point of departure.

The last part of the book is called "Points of Arrival." This is about the flowering of the spiritual life, not so much as I could claim to have experienced it personally, but as I have observed it in others and increasingly understand it myself, as my contemporaries and I begin to grow old, as gracefully as we can.

Perhaps we can never hear our own story clearly, or understand it in depth, until we have heard somebody else's story as well. So it is that we can often discern the action of the Spirit much more clearly in the lives of others than we can in our own lives. The middle part of this book, "Vantage Points," tries to develop a sort of sounding board, a referential perspective, in which or against which readers can measure their own experience of the Spirit.

While the four chapters of this middle part are not autobiographical, each chapter does reflect some aspect of where I am coming from with what I am trying to share with others about the spiritual life: I am a monk, I am a celibate, and I have spent several years in Black Africa. If this is not *my* story, it is nonetheless the story of many people whose testimonies I have heard and seen, testimonies that are largely unheard in our contemporary culture. What readers may perceive, on the surface, as alien to their own experience, or even eccentric, may yet speak to them at a deeper level, helping them to enter into their own stories and to hear them in a new and better way.

> There are varieties of gifts, but the same spirit; and there are varieties of services but the same Lord; and there are varieties of activities, but it is the same God who activates all of them in everyone. (1 Cor 12:4–6)

Saint Benedict says in his rule that "wherever we may be, we are all serving under the same Lord and fighting for the same King" (RB 61:10). It is in this spirit that I offer, along the pilgrim way between our common point of departure and our hoped-for port of arrival, these *ex-centric* vantage points on an itinerary upon which we are all embarked, "this strange adventure which we call human life."[2]

PART ONE

Points of Departure

CHAPTER ONE

What Must I Do?

What must I do? That question sounds time and again in the Bible, in literature, and in life. What to do is a big issue. Especially if what I do, or don't do, makes a difference, even *the* difference.

The problem, as Hamlet discovered, is not so much about alternative courses of action and the morality of each, nor about willpower, courage, or cowardice. The real question is about the very possibility of meaningful action. The seminary companions of Julien Sorel seek "to perform significant acts."[1] But what are significant acts? Can we do anything that makes a difference? Can we make ourselves or save ourselves, whatever that might mean?

Is not every man Hamlet, and Hamlet each one of us? "Man, haunted man, struggling to get something done as man has struggled from the beginning, yet incapable of achievement because of his inability to understand either himself or his fellows or the real quality of the universe which has produced him."[2]

Throughout history we have journeyed in search of answers: across deserts and seas, up mountains, down holes in the ground, into caves, to all the holy and high places of the planet, to witches and fortune-tellers, and even into churches. We are forever popping our question to whosoever might have an answer: *What must I do?* We have challenged the oracles and philosophers of ancient Greece; the *Abbas* and *Ammas* of Egypt, Syria, and Palestine; the sages of Buddhism, Hinduism, and Islam; the geniuses of the Enlightenment—which is to name but a few. And today, with our bewilderingly various profusion of gurus and therapists: never before have we had so many self-proffering fielders of the question.

Although we are adept at asking questions, we are not always so good at hearing answers. There can be a lot of spiritual maneuvering tied up in asking this particular question. Wheeler-dealers and bargain hunters, we tend to pitch the question in such a way as to preempt the answer. Wouldn't it be nice to wrap up God in a binding contract: heaven in return for some good behavior? Is that, really, what our question is all about?

The Rich Young Man

> As Jesus was setting out on a journey, a man ran up and knelt before him, and asked him, "Good Teacher, what must I do to inherit eternal life?" (Mark 10:17)

The rich young man was manifestly a good boy, one for whom any reasonable contract of service would present no problem. He got a soft answer initially, or so he thought. He did not know Jesus. Jesus radicalizes the Law: You have heard how it was said to our ancestors do this—but I say to you: Love your enemies as well as your friends; forced to go a mile, go two miles; struck on the right cheek, turn the other cheek; robbed of your cloak, offer your coat also; forgive, not just seven times, but seventy times seven. "You must set no bounds to your love, just as your heavenly Father sets no bounds to his" (Matt 5:20–48). It is not long before Jesus opens these perspectives of total commitment to the rich young man.

Jesus, looking at him, loved him and said, "You lack one thing; go sell what you own, and give the money to the poor, and you will have treasure in heaven; then come follow me" (Mark 10:21).

The young man is horrified at this sudden escalation of prices, this leap from quantifiable costs to *everything*, and his own heart and soul as well. "When he heard this, he was shocked and went away grieving, for he had many possessions" (Mark 10:22). Remaining in the cautious perspective of his own question, he does not realize that what he has been offered is not what he asked for—a contract of service—but instead a personal and total relationship, love without reserve or limitation. In this new perspective, the cost is simply irrelevant. *So much rubbish,* Saint Paul says, speaking of all that he had left behind him, everything that had seemed most important, everything that had meant self-image, self-esteem, and even righteousness for him—until he encountered Jesus Christ (Phil 3:7–12).

Jesus is not naming a price. He is inviting the young man, and all of us, to accept an astonishing gift, the incomparable gift of his companionship and love. What must we do? Free our hearts, open our arms to receive. *Learn from me* (Matt 11:29). Then, day by day, we will indeed know what we must do.

Where your treasure is, there is your heart (Matt 6:21). Finding a treasure hidden in the earth, or a pearl of great price, Jesus says, a person will go off *happy* to sell everything and take possession of that pearl, that treasure (Matt

13:44–46). To find one's true treasure is to find one's own heart as well. This is the secret, and the price, of self-discovery, true integration, and maturity: to find our treasure and to go for it.

Know the Gift of God

On the morning of Pentecost, the people asked Peter and the apostles, "Brothers, what should we do?" Peter answered, "Repent, and be baptized every one of you in the name of Jesus Christ so that your sins may be forgiven; and you will receive the gift of the Holy Spirit" (Acts 2:37–38). This is the very definition of conversion, to turn away from reliance on ourselves and from selfishness, and to open our hearts to receive healing and the *gift of the Holy Spirit* (Acts 16:30–34).

When Jesus is asked to heal somebody, he never asks whether that person is worthy, whether he or she is *doing* something worthwhile or keeping the terms of some notional contract. He simply asks, "Do you believe that I can do this for you?" Saint John explains what is asked of us: "This is [God's] commandment, that we should believe in the name of his Son Jesus Christ and love one another" (1 John 3:23–24). To love one another is not a condition of receiving God's love: it is a consequence of that love, an overflowing of the gift that we ourselves have received.

Saint John's Gospel, chapter 6, is a rich and powerful proclamation of God's gift in Jesus Christ. The chapter begins with a bonus of earthly bread, which prompts people interested in securing such practical benefits in the future to ask, "What must we do to perform the works of God?" It is, once again, the contract-of-service perspective. Jesus answers,

"This is the work of God, that you believe in him whom he has sent." In other words, faith *is* the work. The focus of attention is God's gift, not our own moral, doctrinal, or ritual rectitude.

Jesus continues to speak at length, trying to express the extent of the gift that God will bestow on those who open their hearts to receive it, culminating in the self-giving of God himself on Calvary and in the Eucharist. "Whoever eats of this bread will live forever." But some people cannot accept love and gift. They expect and want to be self-made. For them, *What must I do?* is and will remain the vital question. So "because of this many of Jesus' disciples turned back and no longer went about with him."

And Jesus said, "The words that I have spoken to you are spirit and life."

CHAPTER TWO

Let God Be God

God Speaks through Mammy Wagons

The title for this chapter comes from the back of a great lumbering mammy wagon that I got stuck behind one day on the dry dusty road from Benin City to Onitsha, in Nigeria, West Africa.

Impressive vehicles, these mammy wagons, gargantuan trucks with a great wooden cage behind, piled high with tiers of merchandise, minor livestock, and people. They only sometimes topple over or shed their loads, which is in flat contradiction with the laws of gravity. There are no seat-belts, nor even seats, nor any stuffy regulations to restrain happy passengers, perched astride bags and bales high above the protective barrier of wooden caging, from falling off. The passengers never do. One hand, if even, holds on, the other is kept free for gesticulating, smoking, feeding, or just waving to the timorous European clutching his sweat-sticky steering wheel and being gassed to death by diesel fumes, in the car behind.

In place of the advertising graffiti with which the Western world disfigures vacant surfaces, the owners of mammy wagons have the much better idea of covering them with colorful and often artistic proclamations of their faiths and philosophies. A few samples from an inexhaustibly creative repertoire:

One and God is Majority.
God spare my enemies to see my success.
Money hard: Woman no know!
Better late than the late!
Psalm 22, Amen.

And this one, which Joyce would say, was having an epiphany on the back of that lorry, just as I happened to look up from my sauna-bath steering wheel. It touched my heart like the word of a spiritual father, a gift from the Spirit, and I have never forgotten it: *Let God be God.*

What a really perfect idea! Why do I always insist on steering, on driving the bus? Why am I always trying to overtake? Why am I such an uptight little godling, always center stage in the soap opera of my own life? Even on the rare occasions when I do let God be God, I still behave like his stereotypical mother-in-law, back-seat driving him the whole way.

Peter as Paradigm

Contrast two scenes in the Gospels. Both involve Jesus and Peter. On each occasion, Jesus does something or says something in Peter's presence that Peter experiences as a direct question or challenge to himself. So much so that, each time, it becomes a fundamental issue of whether the two can stay together at all, or will each have to go his separate way.

Luke 5:4–8

The first scene is when Jesus, who has been preaching from Peter's boat on the Lake of Gennesarat, challenges him to "put out into deep water." This phrase can be interpreted both literally, in navigational terms, and spiritually, as an invitation to a daunting and dangerous commitment. Peter obeys, literally; he puts out into deep water. The result is a haul of fish so great that the fishermen's nets are almost tearing.

Then Peter, so accustomed to skippering his own boat, is overcome with dread. He is losing control. He realizes incoherently that what Jesus has done is a direct challenge to himself, that Jesus is claiming him and calling him to a kind of navigation, a commitment, and a way of life in which he will not be in control, and for which he knows he is wholly unsuited and utterly ill equipped. He falls to his knees and earnestly begs Jesus to get out of his boat, and out of his life. "Go away from me, Lord, for I am a sinful man."

Time goes by. Peter has followed Jesus. He is probably still a sinful man. Some of his least glorious moments have yet to come. But, at some level within himself, deeper than morals and performance, he has changed and is still changing. He has grown and is growing.

John 6:67–70

The scene this time is precisely where we finished in chapter 1, at the end of chapter 6 in John's Gospel. People are walking away from Jesus; even his own followers are deserting him. Stuck in the perspective of the works that *they* must do and of the material rewards that God will confer on them as signs of his favor, they remain closed to the real and utterly free gift of God in Jesus Christ.

At this point Jesus turns to his chosen Twelve. This time it is he who raises the possibility of a parting of the ways. "Do you also wish to go away?" They are free, as was that rich young man, to go or to stay. Jesus never forces anybody. Simon Peter answered him, "Lord, to whom can we go? You have the words of eternal life. We have come to believe and know that you are the Holy One of God."

A simple comparison of what Peter said on each of these two occasions is enough to bring out the extent of his spiritual itinerary in the meantime.

"Go away from me, Lord, for *I* am a sinful man."

"Lord, to whom can we go? *You* have the words of eternal life."

The simple change of subject from *I* to *you* says it all. Peter has taken himself out of the central position and put Jesus, the Holy One of God, there instead. He no longer believes that what he, Peter, is—whether sinful or saintly—is the decisive factor. The essential thing is who Jesus Christ is and what God is doing in and through him.

Peter has learned to *let God be God*. In spite of his sinfulness, he will stay with Jesus. His spiritual maturing is the paradigm for all who would follow Christ.

Yes, it does take a long time.

CHAPTER THREE

Who Is Jesus Christ?

Now when Jesus came into the district of Caesarea
Philippi, he asked his disciples "Who do people say
that the Son of Man is?" And they said, "Some say
John the Baptist, but others Elijah, and still others
Jeremiah or one of the prophets." He said to them,
"But who do you say I am?" (Matt 16:13–15)

Modest Beginnings

Half a century ago, when I was being confirmed, it was
the custom for the bishop to pass through the ranks of children, stopping at random here and there to ask questions
about Christian doctrine. If you flunked your question, we
had been warned repeatedly, you were out. What a terrible
disgrace! This was one very big deal.

That morning the bishop advanced at a leisurely pace
through the rows of juvenile theologians, like Nemesis with
time on his hands, picking off victims here and there.
Nobody was seen to slink shame-faced from the church. We
waited in agony nonetheless. As I knew he would, the bishop
stopped when he got to me. "Who is Jesus Christ?"

Shocked silence in heaven for at least half an hour. Then
I heard myself saying in a shaky voice, "Bishop, that question is not in the Catechism!"

More shock and silence, filled now with foreboding about what would be done to me afterward for such incredible cheek. The bishop, who looked quite kindly, was visibly nonplussed himself. In 1948, dialogue in the church had not yet been invented.

Then, to everybody's amazement, that good man began to rummage under his layers of purple, eventually coming up with a battered penny catechism. He flicked through the pages, smiled, and said, "Sorry, son! What does the name Jesus Christ signify?"

I hit that beach running: *"JesussignifiesSaviorChrist signifiesanointedandSaintPaulsaysinthenameofJesus— everykneeshouldbend!"*

He smiled again and said, "You are a good boy." He was wrong about that too.

This all seems amusing now, and even frivolous. And yet, many of our most important insights and experiences come in that sort of incongruous or even slightly absurd situation.

Who is Jesus Christ? The question disconcerted me then mightily by not being in the catechism. Obliged, however briefly, to confront the substance and not merely the formula, I was totally at sea. The peril was not just social or disciplinary. It was as if I had glimpsed something mysterious and dangerous that a child should not see, like sex or death. Fifty-five years later, that question still disconcerts me because I still do not really know the answer.

Who Do You Say That I Am?

It is a question addressed to each one of us, every day: "Who do you say that I am?" It disconcerts us, or it should. This is not a guessing game, a theology quiz, or some bland exercise in erudition. The disciples did not answer Jesus with the formulas of Nicaea or Chalcedon, or even with the penny catechism. They could not have, and neither can we, even if we know those answers.

What we are asked for is not a formula, a theory, or a slogan, but a conversion and a commitment, a willingness to follow and to be changed utterly. It is who Jesus Christ is that defines me. Because of who he is, I must change; I must leave this place and follow him, perhaps where I would rather not go (John 21:18).

Knowledge, theology, even faith: none of these is enough. The demons know and believe, and they tremble (Jas 2:19). Physical vision is not enough either. Many people saw and heard Jesus. Some were superficially excited, moved with the sterile faith that calls out, "Lord, Lord," but goes no further. He will tell them to their faces, "I have never known you" (Matt 7:23). Others who saw Jesus were plainly disappointed. Herod saw only a fool (Luke 23:11), and Pilate, staring, with *The Truth* inches from his nose, asked petulantly, "What is truth?" (John 18:38).

Paul says, "Even though we once knew Christ from a human point of view, we know him no longer in that way" (2 Cor 5:16). Indeed, it is necessary for Jesus to go away from our fleshly, and even from our intellectual and psychological grasp, in order for the Spirit to come, through whom alone we can truly know Christ (John 16:7; Rom 8:9). After the resurrection, the disciples who see Jesus do not recognize him. Some word or gesture of his is necessary to reveal him to us: he breaks bread (Luke 24:30), calls our name (John 20:16), or speaks to us directly (John 21:4–7).

The gift of this *word* is the lifeline of true faith. Faith is not a question of having a more gullible nature or a livelier imagination than anybody else, or of having antennae—we need to beware of people with antennae. Nor is faith a matter of being a feistier gambler than others, calculating the odds on a god existing and on Jesus being that god.[1]

When Jesus says, "Blessed are those who have not seen and yet have come to believe" (John 20:29), he is not praising the extreme elasticity of the disciples' believing powers: he is celebrating the blessedness of those who have received the word of God as gift and treasured it.

> Although you have not seen him, you love him; and even though you do not see him now, you believe in him and rejoice with an indescribable and glorious joy, for you are receiving the outcome of your faith, the salvation of your souls. (1 Pet 1:8–9)

People are surprised that they cannot pray—as if prayer were a democratic right that any normal well-adjusted person should be able to exercise as routinely as they ride a bicycle. If it seems not to be working, and they cannot pray, they may go looking for another book, a new method or technique, better breathing exercises, more mystical music or incense. But prayer and faith itself are not primarily about skills or well-crafted experiences: they are pure gift, without which we cannot even say, "Jesus is Lord" (1 Cor 12:3). "For what human being knows what is truly human except the human spirit that is within? So also no one comprehends what is truly God's except the Spirit of God" (1 Cor 2:11).

Just as faith is not founded on human philosophy but on the power of God, so the prayer and good works that flow from faith are "a demonstration of the Spirit and of power" (1 Cor 2:5). Here too, here especially, we must let God be

God. The foundation and dynamic of our Christian faith and life is not that *we* have come to acknowledge God, but that *he* constantly acknowledges and affirms us (Gal 4:9). Our contribution is to accept the gift of God (John 4:10) with gratitude and humility.

Jesus said, "No one comes to the Father except through me" (John 14:6). We know that. But he also said, "No one can come to me unless he is drawn by the Father who sent me" (John 6:44). To Peter, who acknowledged him as "Christ and Son of the living God," he said, "Blessed are you, Simon, son of Jonah! For flesh and blood has not revealed this to you, but my Father in heaven" (Matt 16:17).

The spirit of à la carte Christianity, of choosing what seems right *for me,* or what *I* feel comfortable with, puts all the accents in the wrong places. Our personal integrity, sincerity, and authenticity are, of course, important, but the Word of God is even more fundamental and true. Christ is the rock on which the church is built (Matt 16:18)—not my self-understanding or self-esteem, and still less, my self-importance. The idea of the church as a sum total, or a lowest common denominator, of individualisms is a nonsense. The Word of God is not comfort food, or just another therapy. It is "living and active, sharper than any two-edged sword…able to judge the thoughts and intentions of the heart" (Heb 4:12–13).

To let God be God is to make myself vulnerable. It is to pray, "Speak, Lord: your servant is listening!" rather than "Listen, Lord: your servant is speaking!" It is to be much less sure of myself. It is to want to hear and obey the Word of God. It is to need the sacraments. It is to journey beyond narcissism toward what is real, objective, and true. It is to embark on the exciting and alarming work of conversion. It is to begin to know Jesus Christ.

CHAPTER FOUR

Approaches to the Mystery of Jesus

A First Approach: The Name of Jesus

On the eighth day, the child was circumcised and received his name, Jesus. The eighth day is the octave day of Christmas. So it came about, in the Western world at least, that the octave day of Christmas became the beginning of the New Year. It is a happy omen to begin the New Year on this day, when the child Jesus received his name, the only name by which we can be saved (Matt 1:21; Acts 4:12). The name *Jesus, Yehoshua* in Hebrew, means "Yahweh saves."

In the ancient world, the giving of a name was very important. There are many examples of this in the Bible. The name, especially when given by God, told people who this person was to become and what he or she was destined to accomplish. So Abram became Abraham, Jacob became Israel, Simon became Peter the rock. The name also told the person himself or herself who he or she was. That, surely, was important too. *Know thyself* is the first precept of ancient and of perennial wisdom.

The creation story tells us that God brought all the creatures he had made and paraded them before Adam so that Adam would name them. In naming them, the man

17

identified and even decided what each creature was to be. When this inventory had been completed, it became apparent that no equal or companion for man was to be found (Gen 2:20).

Although we can assign roles and labels to each other, only God can make and name a human person, man or woman. God alone can give us our intimate personal identity, our secret name that even we ourselves only begin to know gradually, as life unfolds. We shall not know that name perfectly until we see ourselves reflected in God, in whose image we are made (Rev 2:17).

This child is called Jesus, which means "Savior." It is, of course, Mary who gives the name, because she was the one to whom it was first entrusted at the Annunciation. It is she, in a sense, who holds the secret of who Jesus is and what he is to accomplish. She treasured that name and all these things and pondered them in her heart, Luke tells us that, and he will repeat it (Luke 2:19,51). Mary is the one who carried in her womb, in her arms, and most especially in her heart the One whose name is above every name (Phil 2:9).

Think of the names that the Angel gave to Mary: *Favored one* and *You who have found favor with God* (Luke 1:28,31). Think of the name that Elizabeth gives jointly to Jesus and Mary: *Blessed One.* "Blessed are you among women, and blessed is the fruit of your womb...and blessed is she who believed that there would be a fulfillment of what was spoken to her by the Lord" (Luke 1:42,45).

The day a child is named is in a special way the mother's day. It is fitting that the day when Jesus received his name should be celebrated in the liturgy of the church as the Solemnity of Mary, Mother of God.

A Second Approach:
Incarnation and Faith

The incarnation is not just another word for the nativity. The nativity is the Christmas event, the birth of Jesus Christ at Bethlehem. The incarnation, on the other hand, is not a single chronological event, one in a series of happenings making up the life story of Jesus Christ: it is the secret melody, the golden thread running through *all* the events of Christ's life, from his conception to his death, from his first infant cry at Bethlehem to that last great cry with which he yielded up his spirit to the Father on Golgotha.

We celebrate the mystery of the incarnation, not just at Christmas, but at all times and in all the feasts of the Lord. We celebrate the incarnation most especially at Easter in the paschal mystery. If the incarnation can be said to have begun at Christmas, or perhaps more correctly at the Annunciation, it is at Easter that it achieves its consummation. Then the Son, going to the extreme limit of human experience, becomes most completely man, and humankind achieves, in him, its apotheosis.

The Son of God, who is eternal and immortal, who is born of the Father before all ages, became a man. He was created in fragile human flesh at a point in history and lived out his eternal sonship of the Father in fleeting time, within the limits of our created, imperfect, and sin-scarred nature. Becoming weak, needy, vulnerable, and mortal, he would one day die. In and through this mystery of the incarnation, the work of our redemption is accomplished, and we are saved.

These expressions—incarnation, redemption, and salvation—are virtually empty of content for our contemporaries.

They belong to the perspective of revelation and faith. They do not stand to reason, in the sense of being logically deductible from some first principle, in the way that idealist philosophers or positivist determinists might like to deduce the whole of human history.

The communication of faith, therefore, is not a matter of boxing nonbelievers into a corner by dint of dialectical skill or moral superiority, even assuming that the churches were liberally endowed with either. Faith is not a series of intellectual propositions to be driven home by argument; nor is it an ethical, social, or political system demonstrably to be preferred to other inferior models.

Yet the church must continue to proclaim the gift of God: Jesus Christ, the Son of God become truly man, our redeemer and savior, the One whose human life is bringing about, through the power of the Spirit, the transfiguration of humanity and the completion of God's work of creation.

If the gospel is indeed "good news," this is precisely because it does not stand to reason; it is not our due, nor is it to be expected. Indeed, it is such very good news as to be startling and almost unbelievable.

A Third Approach: Magic and Miracles

They brought to him a deaf man who had an impediment in his speech; and they begged him to lay his hand on him. He took him aside in private, away from the crowd, put his fingers into his ears and he spat and touched his tongue. Then looking up to heaven, he sighed: and said to him, "Ephphatha," that is, "be opened." And immediately his ears were opened, his tongue was released, and he spoke plainly. (Mark 7:31–37)

What is the difference between some run-of-the mill wizard and Jesus Christ? One does magic and the other works miracles. There is a difference. That is why, in this story about the cure of a deaf and dumb person, Jesus takes the man away from the crowd and cures him in private. He does not want to be mistaken for Harry Potter or some Hogwarts wizard.[1] *Ephphatha* is not a magic word; it is a simple command given with authority: *Be opened.*

Jesus does not use a wand. He puts his finger in the man's ears and says, "Be opened." The finger in the language of the Bible means the power of God. When on Mount Sinai, God wrote the Law on slabs of stone, the Bible says that he wrote it with his finger, emblazoning it into the solid rock as if with fire (Exod 31:18). And when, in the New Testament, Jesus writes the new law of mercy and forgiveness, he writes it on the stone floor of the Temple, with his finger, which means, with the power and authority of God himself (John 8:6,8).[2]

Jesus said, on another occasion, "If it is by the finger of God that I cast out the demons, then the kingdom of God has come to you" (Luke 11:20).

That is exactly what is happening here. This is the meaning of this cure of the deaf man. Jesus is no conjurer, no *juju* man. By the power of the finger of God, he drives out the demon of sadness and isolation that comes with deafness. He heralds the coming of the kingdom that will bring into our deaf-dumb world beautiful sound, music, the word, the possibility of communication and relationships, understanding, and love.

But the story does not finish there. What else does Jesus do? He takes saliva from his own tongue and mouth, and puts it into the mouth and onto the tongue of the deaf-dumb man, again with his finger. That probably strikes us as disgusting. In our postmodern, hygiene-obsessed culture, it is either downright yucky, or else something very intimate to do. We might think of lovers doing something like that.

This happens when we receive communion: Jesus does not merely touch us with the tip of his finger, or put in our mouths drops of his spittle. We take in our hands, we receive in our mouths and on our tongues, we welcome into our bodies, into our most intimate heart and soul, Jesus Christ himself, our brother, our lover, and our God.

Then our ears are opened to hear the melody of the Spirit in our hearts, in the church, and in the world; our eyes are opened to gaze on the wonders of God's work, but also to see the misery and the deprivation of so many of our brothers and sisters. So do we discover the vocation to share love: our hands are raised and strengthened to bring healing and help; our mouths are opened and our tongues are loosened to sing God's praises and to celebrate the magic and the mystery of life and love.

A Fourth Approach: Nazareth and Bethlehem

Nazareth and Bethlehem,
Birth of Jesus: birth of Mary,
Mysteries inseparable
For Jesus is Son of God and Son of Mary.

Born before all time in the image of the Father,
Jesus is born in time in the image of his Mother.
Not two images: one and the same.

Son of the Father, Jesus mirrors perfectly
The uncreated beauty of God.
Created in the image of her Son,
Full of grace, free from every shadow of evil,
Mary is bathed in beauty from the first moment of her being,
In the perfect beauty of God's own self

Created in the image of the Son, all fair,
That the Son might be born most beautiful
Of all the sons of women.

By nature and by nurture, in body and soul,
      in temperament,
Morally, spiritually, Jesus receives from his mother,
      like every son,
And more than any.

At Bethlehem, at Nazareth, at Cana, always, on Calvary
      and beyond,
Forever and to all eternity, Jesus is the Son of Mary.

Through grace and gift, Mary is consecrated to lavish on
      her Son
What she herself has received. Sinless, full of grace, Mary
      mediates to her child
That perfect image of God's beauty which the Holy Trinity
      created within her.

Mary treasures all these things in her heart while Jesus
grows in the loving radiance
Of her presence, in wisdom, in stature, and in grace before
God and men.

Through the gentle mothering of Mary, may the Christ
. Child grow to full stature
In the heart and soul of each one of us.

CHAPTER FIVE

Conversion: The Project

The word *conversion* comes from the Latin *convertere*, meaning "to turn toward" something or somebody, even to turn right around with a view to looking or going in the opposite direction. In religious terms, this could be a radical choice, as when an adult asks for baptism, or a dramatic Damascus experience that launches a person unexpectedly on a new and even contrary itinerary to the one that he or she had been following.

Conversion can also mean the daily, hourly, minute-by-minute tiny touches to the steering wheel or handlebars whereby we preempt or correct the tendency to stray off course. This is the *metanoia* of the ancient monks, the habit of thinking again and thinking better about what we are doing, saying, or allowing to dominate our thoughts in the present moment.

The two aspects are inseparable. *Metanoia*, which means literally "change of mind," is a fundamental transformation of attitude, the adoption of a new perspective or preoccupation. But it is also the deep desire and ongoing struggle to be consistent and undivided in our loyalty to this new vision or value. Jesus said, "Where your treasure is, there your heart will be also" (Matt 6:21). True integration of the whole person is achieved gradually, according as one arrives, through a long process of conversion, at this undividedness of heart. This integrity is what scripture calls "purity of heart."

Purity of Heart

In the narrower spirituality of a later age, the word *purity* came to be associated almost exclusively with sexual morality, but when Jesus said, "Blessed are the pure in heart, for they will see God" (Matt 5:8), he was talking about an integrity of soul that extends not just to sexuality but also to all aspects of a person's thinking, feeling, and desiring. Similarly for the psalmist, when he prayed, "A pure heart create for me, O God, put a steadfast spirit within me" (Ps 51:10). That steadfastness of spirit is the same thing as purity of heart. It is purity in the sense of *simply and solely,* like when we speak of *pure* gold or *pure* oil. We mean unadulterated, authentic, the real thing and nothing else. Jesus said, "Martha, Martha, you are worried and distracted by many things; there is need of only one thing" (Luke 10:41). To be pure of heart is to have, like Mary, "chosen the better part."

The desert fathers of the fourth and fifth centuries envisaged monastic life—and, more fundamentally, Christian life itself—as a long journey from dividedness and alienation back to integration of the person and purity of heart. So it is that John Cassian, in *The Conferences,* although he identifies the kingdom of God as our ultimate goal, goes on to insist that our immediate goal is purity of heart, without which it is impossible for anyone to reach the ultimate goal (Conf. 1:4).

Some of the desert fathers offer wonderfully joyful portraits of those who do finally achieve purity of heart, often depicting such people as having returned to the paradisiacal state even in this life. So it is that Abba Paul of the Thebaïd said, "If somebody has obtained purity, everything is in submission to him, as it was to Adam, when he was in paradise before he disobeyed."[1] In the same way, Evagrius wrote, "Like a morning star in heaven and a palm tree in paradise, so is a pure mind in a gentle soul."[2] Gentleness is one of the surest signs that a person has attained to purity of heart.

When anger and violence, together with all the other disordered passions, have been overcome, a person achieves perfect harmony within himself and with all creation. So it is that Saint Athanasius describes Anthony the Great, the first desert hermit, as dying at the age of 105, still looking extraordinarly youthful, and still possessed of all his teeth! Typically, in these delightful stories, snakes and wild beasts do no harm to these holy men and women and even run messages and perform other useful services for them.

According to Evagrius, the great fourth-century synthesist of desert spirituality, it is the pure of heart, now living in profound harmony with God, with their fellow humans, and with all creation, who can really penetrate the deep mysteries of nature. Evagrius is not thinking about science or technology in the narrow sense: he is talking about a contemplative understanding of everything in the unifying light of God.

But this is the happy ending to a long labour of conversion. Purity of heart is not the point of departure: it is the distant horizon. Columba Stewart quotes with approval the words of Flannery O'Connor, "The phrase *naïve purity* is a contradiction in terms. I don't think that purity is mere innocence; I don't think that babies and idiots possess it. I take it to be something that comes with experience or with Grace so that it can never be naïve."[3]

Stewart also points out that the Greek word *katharos,* used in early spiritual writing and translated "pure," actually means "purified"; it comes from a verb meaning "to take away," and thus "to cleanse." The starting point is messiness and confusion.

Spiritual Warfare

Jesus said, "For out of the heart come evil intentions: murder, adultery, fornication, theft, false witness, slander. These are what defile a person" (Matt 15:19). Whatever way we understand the mystery of evil, whether we talk about original sin, using mythological narratives about a primeval fall, or whether we prefer the equally mythological language of modern psychology, with its Oedipal conflicts, superegos, and archetypes, our starting point has got to be the recognition of a deep dividedness and struggle within ourselves.

Whether or not we have a good theory about the origins of negativity within our unconverted hearts, whether or not we have found somebody or something to blame for it, that evil is a pragmatic fact that has to be faced. Anybody of good sense and even short experience knows that it is just not enough to say, either to oneself or to others, "Go with your feelings, follow your instincts, let it all hang out, do what you feel comfortable with." Any educational project based solely on such premises would certainly lead to disaster. Sooner or later, we have got to acknowledge that we have some nasty instincts and more than trivial problems of selfishness, laziness, and lack of honesty, even, or most especially, with ourselves. This is where the work of conversion and the journey toward purity of heart must begin.

Thought, or the lack of it, is, of course, the key to so much of what we do or say. This is why the ancient masters of the spiritual life attached so much importance to vigilance over one's thoughts and the need to make one's habitual thought patterns known to one's spiritual guide. When we say "thought" and "thought patterns," it is not just a question of something coldly intellectual. What is at issue is that inseparable mixture of thoughts, feelings, and desires that affects our attitudes and behavior, and especially our treatment of other people for better or for worse.

There are some therapies today that, though useful in their own way, tiptoe around the essential issues of mental and spiritual hygiene. Whatever emotional or psychological wounds we may have suffered in life—and probably none of us has escaped entirely unscathed—there is nevertheless a level at which we must take responsibility for ourselves, recognizing our need for conversion and accepting that we have some, or even many, unpleasant thought patterns, attitudes, and instinctive reactions that, however damaged we may be, we still can and need to do something about, if we want to grow humanly and spiritually.

The *Logismoi*

This strange word, variously translated as "thoughts," "feelings," "fantasies," "urges," "temptations," and even "demons," is typically used by the desert fathers to describe the inseparable mixture of thoughts, feelings, desires, passions, imaginings, and delusions that make up our inner lives, and that powerfully affect, and even determine, our attitudes toward God, our neighbors, and ourselves. The fathers spoke of *thoughts* when they wanted to stress that all this inner activity of mind and heart is coming from within ourselves and that we have got to take responsibility for it. On the other hand, they spoke of *demons,* who have somehow managed to insinuate themselves into our minds and feelings, when they wished to acknowledge that we are not inherently bad and that evil does, in some sense, come from outside ourselves.

When I was a youngster, we were often warned against "bad thoughts." This invariably meant lustful fantasies, or so we thought anyhow. Nobody, that I can recall, ever warned us against angry, envious, self-pitying, or megalomaniac daydreams, which is a pity. In all of those areas, too, the advice of Evagrius would have been apt and valuable: "Do not let a scorpion linger on your breast, nor in your heart an evil thought!" (*Ad Mon.* 58).

Evagrius seems to have been the first to codify and write down the wisdom of the desert fathers on the subject of the principal thoughts or demons that assail our minds and hearts.

There are eight of these *logismoi.* The first three attack the desiring part of the soul. The next three target the reactive or irascible faculties. The last and most dangerous two are aimed at the purely spiritual part of the soul. This is hardly the way we would carve up the soul or the *psyche* nowadays, nor does this list of enemies of the soul correspond with current ideas about what might be healthy or harmful in the inner life of thoughts and feelings. The desert model is nonetheless valuable and probably as good as any other inventory or catalog. At the present time, it does have the advantage of sounding some alarm bells in the general complacency of our contemporary, nonjudgmental—not to say amoral—appraisal of the inner world of thought, feeling, and fantasy. Here is the list of the *logismoi,* with a few brief comments on each.[4]

Gluttony

This extends to the whole area of swallowing, including what we would now call "oral satisfaction": excessive eating and drinking, smoking, and, by extension, all forms of substance abuse, and possibly certain forms of sexual perversion. The element of quick-fix compensation in compulsive or binge consumption is well recognized. Such behavior is unwise, to say the least. Is it really *evil?* Subjectively, probably not, in a context of compulsion and obsession. In a context of freedom and the opportunity to grow spiritually, it *is* evil, and we should acknowledge this, at least to ourselves, whenever we overindulge.

Obesity and other unhealthy conditions associated with overindulgence and substance abuse have reached epidemic proportions in Western society. This is not just a flat pragmatic fact: it is a significant *spiritual* indicator.

Fornication

The word *fornication* is used in a broad sense to cover all sexual self-indulgence that is unloving and depraved. There is a clear distinction between sex and lust. The first is good in all its aspects, erotic and spiritual. The second is always a perversion and a degradation of persons.

Far from being obsessed about sexual sins, the desert fathers regarded them as signs of immaturity, or else as symptoms of some other, more deep-seated spiritual problem. They also suggested that God sometimes leaves people weak in this area or allows them to regress unexpectedly into some embarrassing fault or habit, so as to humble them, thus shielding them from much more serious sins of arrogance or pride.

Avarice

This is love of money or of what money can buy. It is excessive dependence on possessions and preoccupation with luxury and comfort. The real mischief here is to allow mere things to be the foundation for one's self-esteem and security and the basis for one's relationship with others. It is impossible to acquire purity of heart and knowledge of God if the heart is enslaved to tawdry status symbols and trinkets.

Sadness

Finding ourselves, on the one hand, deprived and frustrated in respect of all these more or less physical desires, and on the other hand, still far from intimacy with God, we become disappointed, resentful, and full of self-pity. Everything saddens us, not least the apparent contentment and success of everybody else. We seem to have lost everything we had before we embarked on the spiritual life and gained nothing in return. It seems that nobody loves little me—and especially not God!

This sadness is quite different from both clinical depression, which is a medical condition, and the dark nights of the soul, which belong to the mystical life and are anything but self-centered.

Anger

Frustration turns to anger. The spiritual fathers talk more about anger than about any other disease of the soul. It is perhaps the most widespread and the greatest obstacle of all to spiritual progress. Cassian is emphatic that anger is *never* justified, not even in a good cause. Dorotheos of

Gaza, otherwise quite a disciplinarian, is equally sure that it is better to leave vices uncorrected than to correct them in anger. And Evagrius sums it up in maxims that have all the ring of lived experience: "Better a gentle worldly man than an irascible and wrathful monk!" (*Ad Mon.* 34), and "A small-souled old man, who will be able to stand him?" (*Ad Mon.* 112).

In these days of fractured relationships, road rage, savage sexual crimes, violence of every kind, and so much depression, which is clearly anger turned in against oneself, nobody needs to be alerted to the spiritual ravages of anger.

Acedia

The word *acedia* means "radical boredom." It is to be discontented, ungrateful, and fed up with life. The fathers sometimes identified this frame of mind with the *Noonday Devil* of Psalm 90. Life is empty and pointless. Nothing ever happens. No challenge engages the heart. We can settle down to nothing. One's inner life is a bad joke. Spiritually, we feel that we have missed the boat, and that there won't be another sailing. We settle down to a life of listless mediocrity.

The spiritual remedies for this sad condition are to engage in regular but not compulsive work, to pray humbly and with hope, to be compassionate toward others and, above all, to stand and fight, not to tire and run away. "Stay in your cell," the fathers used to say; "it will teach you everything." Sound advice in these days of shallow commitment and highly commercialized escapism.

Vain Glory

This is to hunger for human praise and to revel in it, to prefer one's own glory to God's glory, and to despise others. As Cassian points out, this vice presses hardest on its conquerors: The more we overcome it, the more we have to be vain about. It is, as Cassian adds, like an onion: The more we peel it, the more new skins we encounter.

Human company and living in community are the best cure for vain glory. As Cassian points out in *The Institutes* with deadpan humor, community is like a good laundry washing very dirty clothes: it *boils* the faults out of us—and vain glory especially (Inst. 8:18). Marriage does the same. Dostoevsky says somewhere that only great men's wives fail to take them seriously. I used to quote this saying sometimes when giving retreats, until I noticed how many men applied it, without a flicker of humor, to their own situations.

Pride

If vain glory is a sort of escapism, in which we preen ourselves on the quality of our performance in some or many areas, pride is a radical idolatry of self, an arrogant independence in respect of God and man. Spiritual pride, Cassian says, is "unknown to the majority and beyond their experience....We who are still entangled in earthly passions are not fit to be tempted in this way, but in a more basic way we are undermined by the joy of the flesh, so to speak" (Inst. 12:24). In this we are surely fortunate, because spiritual pride, which pits the creature against God himself, is truly demonic.

There is also a fleshly pride characteristic of spiritual beggars on horseback. Cassian gives a satirical picture of the

monk afflicted by this disease, which is by no means con-
fined to monks and monasteries; others may readily recognize the acuteness of his observation:

> Tepid and ill-instructed, disobedient and rude, not
> gentle and affable, nor at ease with his brethren,
> brash when he talks, sullen when he remains silent,
> elated and overwhelming when he is cheerful, unrea-
> sonably morose when he is depressed, bitter when
> questioned, glib when talkative, prolific in verbiage
> without any in-depth consideration, he knows noth-
> ing of patience, a stranger to charity, argumentative,
> slow to obey except where his own preference and
> will are in agreement, disagreeable when receiving
> correction, soft at restraining his own desires, unwill-
> ing to submit to others, always wanting to make his
> own terms, never prepared to give in to what others
> want. In short he is incapable of listening to advice
> that might save him, but in all matters prefers his
> own judgement to that of his superior. He longs to
> dwell in a cell alone, or indeed to found a monastery,
> and is even eager to collect people to teach and train
> himself. (Inst. 12:25–30, condensed)

Cassian would have made an excellent novelist. He is
particularly good at these pen-pictures depicting accurately
how people who are not eager to face the truth about themselves can deteriorate steadily, sinking further all the time
into self-illusion and fatuity. The irony is that the more other
people see the truth about such a person, the less that person
becomes capable of seeing it themselves.

Logismoi for Today

It would be easy to lengthen the desert list of *logismoi*, which, of course, formed the basis for the familiar catalog of seven deadly sins attributed to Pope Saint Gregory the Great. Envy and jealousy would certainly have to be added. Envy, in particular, was well known to the early fathers. Saint Cyprian makes of it "the root of all evils," and Cassian regards it as especially dangerous because it is "the hidden snake bite" that leaves no surface mark that can be seen and treated. Very few people will admit, even to themselves, that they are consumed by envy. So the disease runs rampant and is very difficult to cure. We have only to look at contemporary Western society to be convinced: envy has become a way of life, almost an art form, if not actually a religion.

The Root of Evil

All of these negative ways of thinking and feeling have in common that they work on our self-love and on our incapacity to trust God and others to love us as much, as exclusively, and as effectively as we love ourselves. Undermining our trust in love, our evil thoughts, if we allow them, lead us farther and farther from reality into an unreal world of insecurity, discontent, anxiety, irrational fears, and pitiable compensations. Simon Tugwell expresses it well:

> All these thoughts have a common element, in that they all derive from self-love. And they all also involve a wrong notion of God. In fact, they all trap us into living in a false human world, wrongly structured around ourselves, and leading to a wrong God.[5]

There are serious reasons for believing that the root of evil, the primordial sin, is not so much pride, or envy, or love of money, or any of the individual *logismoi* but, more fundamentally, the refusal to believe in love and to allow God to be God.

> The woman said to the serpent, "We may eat of the fruit of the trees in the garden; but God said, "You shall not eat of the fruit of the tree that is in the middle of the garden, nor shall you touch it, or you shall die." But the serpent said to the woman, "You will not die; for God knows that when you eat of it your eyes will be opened, and you will be like God, knowing good and evil." (Gen 3:2–5)

It is easy to understand what the tempter is saying: he means that God is not to be trusted, because he loves us too little. He means that we must *not* allow God to be God, because he will surely deprive us of something that would make us happier and more fulfilled. He means that the wisdom of life is to do things *my* way, not God's way.

If our relationship with God is not one of love and trust, it can only be, at best, one of servility and fear, of buying off a power that might otherwise harm us. *What must I do?* becomes a question of finding out what God wants—bottom line, God's lowest price—and doing the deal. Only a real conversion can wean us away from this sterile and self-alienating way of thinking and lead us to discover God's love and our own true selves.

CHAPTER SIX

Conversion: The Grace

In the previous chapter about ongoing conversion, much was said about the many good and bad habits that need to be respectively cultivated or eliminated. It must seem paradoxical, then, to insist that conversion is not essentially a matter of improving our morals or performing better—desirable though that might be—nor is it a program for making ourselves whatever our tyrannical superegos dictate that we ought to become.

Conversion is not about improving our self-image by getting morally bigger and better each day. In fact, as happened in Saint Paul's case, true conversion brings a considerable measure of self-acceptance and a gradual loss of interest in judging ourselves, let alone others (Phil 3:9–14).

There is not much chance, one might think, of overstressing moral or ascetical effort in our contemporary self-indulgent society. Perhaps not, although perfectionism is itself but another form of self-indulgence. There is every indication that we overrate personal achievement, fulfilment in the form of self-creation, relentless pursuit of an essentially narcissistic perfection—if not moral, yet physical, intellectual, aesthetic, and even mystical. By *mystical* I understand the most dangerous mirage of all: avidity for an illusory experience of God that is, in fact, totally solipsistic, an infernal hall of mirrors.

There are two dangers to such self-centered projects of conversion. The first is that the effort will not succeed; the second, and greater danger, is that it will. If we do not get where we want to go in the business of self-perfection, we may settle down to one of the middle-belt *logismoi:* sadness, anger, or acedia. According to Cassian's sardonic estimation, monasteries are full of such crestfallen people, those who never quite made it to the lofty heights of sanctity, or even much farther than the foothills. If, on the other hand, our project of self-creation does succeed, we are in real danger from the worst of the *logismoi:* vain glory and pride. Mercifully, God routinely smashes all the idols, including our beautiful illusions about ourselves.

As Saint Augustine famously discovered, true conversion is not primarily about ourselves at all, because love of *the other* is the only motive force sufficient to change us and to empower us to change ourselves. This point is central to everything else in this book: Love is never a conquest, it is always a gift. For a Christian, conversion is to come progressively to know Christ Jesus, to lay hold of him, or rather, as Saint Paul corrects himself, to allow him to lay hold of us (Phil 3:12). He is the one to whom we convert, to whom we turn.

The days of our life have been prolonged. (Prol. 36)

True conversion takes a long time. The Synoptic Gospels emphasize the slowness of the first disciples to believe, their obtuseness, their sheer impenetrability. Mark, in particular, stresses that, even after so long in the company of Jesus, the disciples' minds and hearts remained closed to who he really is and what he desired of them and for them (Mark 6:52; 8:17).[1] Where Matthew depicts Peter acknowledging Jesus as "the Son of the living God" (Matt 16:16), Mark will allow him to recognize Jesus only as "the Messiah" (Mark 8:29). For Mark, the demons are the only ones who know who Jesus is, and they have to be silenced because the half-converted disciples are not ready or able to cope with such knowledge.

As Jesus takes the road to Calvary, he is followed by disciples who are still arguing about which of them is the greatest; who want to call down fire and brimstone on anyone who offends them; who rejoice, not in the work of the kingdom, but in the power that has been given them over demons; and who are spoiling for a fight with the Romans.

Especially, their minds are closed to the *kenosis,* to the idea of a Christ who will lay down his life and die. Jesus opens his heart to them about this, but they do not want to know—except Judas, the realist, who sees the writing on the wall and decides that, if this is going to happen, he might as well salvage whatever profit he can from the catastrophe. It is no big deal—in either sense—he is merely selling out on someone who seems determined to sell out on himself.

This is the oft-repeated tragedy of the unconverted human heart. There are no big moral issues for such people, just unfortunate and awkward situations to be turned to best account.[2] This is how holocausts come to happen, whether in Nazi Germany, in Rwanda, or in Kosovo.

John records Jesus as saying that, when he is lifted up, he will draw all people to himself (John 12:32). In Mark's Gospel, the first person to acknowledge Jesus as Son of God is the gentile centurion who stood before the cross and saw him lifted up and die (Mark 15:39). Mark seems to be saying that we must follow Jesus the whole way to Calvary, we must come to the cross personally before we can really believe, understand, and be converted. Until then, and even now, we may still be little more than half-converted pagans.

The Peter Paradigm

The evangelists all see Peter's story as paradigmatic, as the pattern of our slow advance toward conversion. Even after his magnificent confession of faith in Jesus, "You are the Messiah, the Son of the living God," there remains a difficulty, a tension, we could even say a radical disagreement between Jesus and Peter. Perhaps even the word *hostility* might not be too strong. "Get behind me, Satan! You are a stumbling block to me; for you are setting your mind not on divine things but on human things" (Matt 16:23). This is surely the harshest rebuke Jesus addresses to anyone in the entire gospel record.

Peter has understood everything—and nothing. "You will never wash my feet!" he exclaims. He, and perhaps we, cannot bear a God who takes our human condition, to show that the only answer to evil is not power but even greater love, a God who kneels to wash our feet, and who dies an outcast on a cross. Until we accept such a savior, Jesus assures us, we can have no part with him (John 13:8).

Why did Peter deny Christ on the night of his arrest? Was it cowardice? He did lose his courage, but why? Peter was prepared to die with Jesus. He said so vehemently, and he meant it. In the event, he did draw his sword and he did fight, against hopeless odds, until ordered by Jesus to cease. Jesus never accused Peter or the rest of his disciples who would abandon him that night of cowardice. His words were, "You will all become deserters because of me this night" (Matt 26:31). This expression means that the disciples' faith will fail, not their courage. Indeed, the next day, Jesus will tell Pilate, perhaps even with a little pride, that if his kingship were of this world, his men "would be fighting" to prevent his capture (John 18:36).

Peter's problem is that he has never fully committed himself to Christ on Christ's terms, namely that his kingdom is *not* of this world. Peter is half-converted. He has not put on the mind of Christ. He has clung obstinately to his own perspectives down to the bitter end. Brought, at last, face to face with the reality of the cross of Christ, he loses control of everything. Courage, resolve, willpower: all desert him. Nothing can stand that is not built on the rock that is Christ (Matt 16:18).

Jesus had foreseen and foretold this moment. "Simon, Simon, listen! Satan has demanded to sift all of you like wheat, but I have prayed for you that your own faith may not fail; and you, when once you have turned back, strengthen your brothers" (Luke 22:31–32). Faith, belief, and trust in Christ will be the sole foundation of that strength.

Chapter 21 of John's Gospel marks the completion of Peter's conversion. First comes Christ's triple invitation, "Simon son of John, do you love me more than these?" This is followed by Peter's thrice-repeated protestation, "Yes, Lord; you know that I love you." So is the wound of his threefold denial healed and forgiven. Next, indeed interspersed between the three questions and answers, comes the three-times-repeated confirmation of Peter's mission to care for those whom Jesus loves: "Feed my lambs, feed my sheep."

Then come the words in which Jesus foretells "the kind of death by which Peter would glorify God," contrasting the willfulness of the young man and the patient obedience of the mature Peter: "Very truly, I tell you, when you were younger, you used to fasten your own belt and to go wherever you wished. But when you grow old, you will stretch out your hands, and someone else will fasten a belt around you and take you where you do not wish to go."

After this he said to him, "Follow me." These last words, which Jesus will repeat with emphasis—"You are to follow me"—are perhaps the most moving in this intense and tender passage. At the Last Supper, Jesus had said to Peter, "Where I am going you cannot follow me now; but you will follow me afterward." Peter had protested, "Why cannot I follow you now? I will lay down my life for you." Jesus had replied with the brutal truth about an unconverted heart, "Very truly, I tell you, before the cock crows, you will have denied me three times."

Luke tells us that, at the very moment when Peter denied Jesus for the third time, the Lord turned and looked straight at him. "Then Peter remembered the word of the Lord, how he had said to him, 'Before the cock crows today, you will deny me three times,' and he went out and wept bitterly" (Luke 22:61–62).

Is this the moment of conversion: when Peter turns toward his master? No! It is when Jesus turns toward Peter. Now, at last, may Peter truly follow his master.

CHAPTER SEVEN

A Lenten Life

The life of a monk should always have a Lenten
character. (RB 49)

Most people would probably agree with these words of Saint
Benedict.[1] Monks, in the popular imagination, are supposed
to be hollow-cheeked ascetics who eat and drink, sleep and
talk very little. They are also reputed to wear sackcloth and
barbed chains, practice flagellation, and dig a shovelful of
their own graves each day. Monks must be presumed to
derive some job satisfaction or spiritual fulfilment from this
unusual way of life, which would have little attraction for
the average person—except possibly the element of restraint
in food and drink, in the context of keeping fit, looking well,
or performing to one's highest pitch as sportsperson, creative
artist, or risk-taking adventurer.

Those same average people might be surprised to hear
that Saint John Chrysostom insisted that there was, or
should be, no essential difference between monks and
laypeople. They would then be less surprised to learn that
the same saint was eventually chased from his diocese, without too much public outcry in his defense, and left to die of
hardship and neglect.

Benedict wrote his rule some 140 years later. He wrote it
for monks, yet he always regarded the simple gospel message

as the real rule for all Christians, including monks. This is why so much of the rule is relevant to anybody who is open to learn from it. Here, in context, is what Benedict wrote about the Lenten life:

> It is true that the life of a monk should always have a Lenten character, but since few have the strength for this, we urge that all alike should keep their life most pure during these days of Lent and wash away in this holy season the negligence of other times. This can be worthily done if we refrain from all evil behavior and devote ourselves to prayer with tears, to reading and compunction of heart, and to the work of abstinence. In these days, therefore, let us add to the usual measure of our service something by way of personal prayer and abstinence from food and drink, so that each can offer to God, of his own will, something above the measure laid down for him, in the joy of the Holy Spirit. In other words, let each one deny his body some food, drink, loose talk and joking, and look forward to holy Easter with the joy of spiritual longing. (RB 49:1–7)

When Benedict writes, in what is clearly the summation phrase of the whole chapter, that we should "look forward to holy Easter with the joy of spiritual longing," he is not thinking about Easter 539, or whenever next Easter was, as he wrote. He is defining what he understands the whole of monastic life, and indeed of Christian life, to be about. He is explaining what he means by saying at the outset of the chapter that the life of a monk should always have a Lenten character.

Benedict is not advocating a very penitential regime, one so full of mortifications and self-denial that few would have the strength for it. On the contrary, one has the impression that the penitential element is a corrective required during Lent, only because we habitually fall short of something more fundamental at other times. This is clear when Benedict goes on to give examples of the privations he has in mind. There is nothing very terrifying about them. He asks us to "refrain from all evil behavior." He could not decently ask for less. For the rest, he is content to urge each one to choose something that he or she can do freely and joyfully. The examples he then suggests amount to little more than what most sensible people routinely undertake nowadays to preserve psychological balance, good health, and a pleasant appearance, even though Benedict's own motivations would have been more God-centered.

The penitential element in the Lenten life is a preliminary, a corrective to do with freeing oneself for something more important, something that should be central all year-round. The real issue about freedom is not what we need to free ourselves *from* but rather what we want to be free *for*. Without some worthwhile objective, freedom is merely a burden. As dictators everywhere have always understood, people in general are not very interested in freedom. All they really want is "bread and circuses."

Benedict *is* interested in freedom. His Lenten life cuts back on bread and circuses so that, at least for forty days, we can be free to do what we should be doing all the time and every day: looking forward to holy Easter with the joy of spiritual longing. *Pascha expectet*. This expectation is no mere annual ritual: it is the heart of Christian faith. *Expecto Resurrectionem*, we proclaim in the Creed. It is the strong focus of the monk's unwavering hope. "I shall live," he proclaims on the day of his profession, "and you will not disappoint me in my great expectations" (RB 58:21). Benedict bids the monk "to yearn for eternal life with all spiritual longing" (RB 4:46). This phrase is unmistakably parallel with the key expression in the chapter on Lent, "to look forward to holy Easter with the joy of spiritual longing" (RB 49:7b). The monk's longing for Easter is not seasonal. It is perennial.

Expectation, longing, hope: three words epitomizing the inner dynamic of Christian life. It is not surprising, therefore, that Benedict summarizes the entire resources of the monastic "workshop" in the maxim, "Never lose hope in God's mercy" (RB 4:74).

Our culture is short on hope. Living in a Third World country, one is struck by the contrast between the vibrant hope of those who have nothing and the hopelessness of those with too much. There is more spiritual starvation in the Northern Hemisphere of our planet than physical hunger in the poorest parts of the world, and, without doubt, the two phenomena are reciprocally related as cause and effect.

The symptoms of hopelessness are everywhere to be seen in the Western world: addiction, suicide, obsessive greed for everything from food to money, perversion and trivialization of sex, devaluation of marriage and of all enduring personal commitments, crisis in the religious ministry, abdication of parenting—and even of reproduction, to the point of zero growth levels in population, so that, especially in Northern Europe, whole nations have become like colonies of octogenarian lemmings, hobbling headlong into the sea. All of this betokens a society that has massively lost hope.

Of course, hope is dangerous. Hope threatens the precarious security of the present moment, the gratification of bread and circuses *now.* Hope is inseparable from growth, change, and creative insecurity. Hope is for those who travel lightly, risk takers, pilgrims. Our culture craves absolute security now. This is our Achilles' heel. The terrorists have understood that.

Hope is not proactive, which is another difficulty for a society in which people are valued and value themselves in terms of achievement. "What you see is what you get." And what you get is what I am worth. With hope, as opposed to ambition, the center of gravity is elsewhere, and one must wait. Yet hope is not passive; it is not hand-folding resignation. Hope is profoundly dynamic, motivating, and empowering. This conviction lies at the heart of the Easter *kerygma*.

> Blessed be the God and Father of our Lord Jesus Christ. By his great mercy has given us a new birth into a living hope through the resurrection of Jesus Christ from the dead, and into an inheritance that is imperishable, undefiled, and unfading, kept in heaven for you, who are being protected by the power of God through faith....You have not seen him, yet you love him; and even though you do not see him now you believe in him and rejoice with an indescribable and glorious joy, for you are receiving the outcome of your faith, the salvation of your souls. (1 Pet 1:3–9)

This keynote passage from the First Letter of Peter is precisely the perspective of Benedict's Lenten life: looking forward with love, hope, and joy to Easter yet to come. Perhaps the most essential role of Christians has always been, and is today more than ever, to give people hope. "Have your answer ready for people who ask you the reason for the hope that is in you" (1 Pet 3:15).

CHAPTER EIGHT

A Church?

Now the Lord said to Abram, "Go from your country and your kindred and your father's house to the land that I will show you. I will make you a great nation." (Gen 12:1–2)

Perhaps the hardest exodus for us today is to come out of the kindred and comfort of our own individuality, the safeness of our own thoughts and inclinations, to journey toward the *pleroma,* which is Christ in his church.

Institutional or Personal Religion

"The educated person is religious, but against religions." Kathleen Norris[1] amusingly describes the "high emotion" caused when she innocently proposed as a suitable topic for discussion at a literary gathering the question, "What religion were you raised in, and what are you now?" Reactions ranged from embarrassment to open anger.

Institutional religion has a bad name. In 1932, Henri Bergson published a book titled *The Two Sources of Morality and Religion.*[2] His thesis was that there are two kinds of religion: one is social and static, the other is personal and dynamic. Social religion is institutional, churchy religion. It revolves around mandatory beliefs, hierarchies, moral codes, liturgical worship, and ritual practices. Dynamic religion, on the other hand, is personal, interior, and mystical.

If this either/or analysis happened to be correct, we would hardly need to ask which kind of religion seems the more authentic and the more attractive. But the sharp dichotomy between outside and inside is too neat. So many of the great mystics have been men and women of the institutional church, nourished by its scriptures, by its community, its sacraments, its liturgy, and its disciplined life. If Edmund Burke was correct in defining man as a "religious animal," we would need to remember that this animal is neither angel nor pure spirit. We are physical and social beings. A religion that is purely personal, interior, and spiritual is less than wholly human. By the same token, it could never be the religion of the incarnation.

And yet, institutional religion is uncongenial in our own day. We can blame the deplorable behavior of some clerics, which has been so exhaustively chronicled and castigated in the media. We may feel that this media coverage has sometimes been unfair and unbalanced,[3] but there is an awareness within the church that some of our gravest problems have sprung from insensitivity, callousness, and even usurpation of the spiritual and emotional integrity of persons still seeking themselves and the truth of their own lives. The most shocking examples of this have been the episodes of sexual abuse of children and teenagers. But the sheer sordidness of those cases should not obscure from us the underlying and more generalized problem: the misuse of power within the institutional church in areas that impinge upon the dignity and integrity of individual persons.

Spiritual Cave-Dwellers

It is told of Saint Benedict, the founder of the religious family to which I belong, that while still a teenager and in the early flush of religious enthusiasm, he went off to become a hermit and lived for upward of three years in a cave, mistaken for a wild animal by those who caught occasional glimpses of him. He did not, in so far as we can judge from his life story,[4] belong to any Christian community, receive the sacraments or even go to mass during all that period.

This loner, a-liturgical, Benedict might appeal to the spiritual cave-dwellers of our own day—those who, although they truly seek God, do it elsewhere than in their own local churches. Skeptical, or at least not attracted by organized religion, they do not look to pastors or congregations for help in working out a personal spirituality. For such people, Benedict the cave-dweller could indeed be patron and paradigm, an acceptable face of the church. Although in later life he himself discouraged others tempted to emulate his premature enthusiasm for eremetical living, it is precisely in the inchoateness and *ex-centricity* of his youthful ardor that many young people today might find him attractive and strangely contemporary.

Few nowadays will want to live physically in caves, but mentally, morally, and spiritually, many already do. Impervious to, even repelled by, the preaching and practice of the churches—which, to be fair, are often perceived through the skewed images of a shallow culture—such people may be "driven by the Spirit into the wilderness" (Mark 1:12) for a period of struggle and discernment.

Those driven by the Spirit need more than safe conformity, more than docile routine, whether in synagogue, parish, monastery, or cave. This is the real drama of empty churches today, not the defection to Mammon or to obsessive triviality of the spiritually moribund, but the disengagement of the spiritually alive, of many who do seek and are driven to seek, not just a regimen of spiritual exercises, but a challenge and an art of spiritual living. For such as these, the cave, physical or metaphorical, may be a necessary initiation into that spiritual art.

The first step toward the church, or back toward the church, can be when a cave-dweller is attracted to a Christian community, a church, perhaps a monastery, as to a place where "spiritual warfare is being fought, not by mercenaries or by slaves who are being forced to fight, but by free people who rejoice in their freedom."[5] That freedom is essential to those driven by the Spirit, as much in our own day as it was in Benedict's time. Was it not he who, hearing that Martin the Hermit had chained himself to a rock in his cave, sent an urgent message that the love of Christ alone should bind us, rather than chains of iron.

Paradoxically, it is often the cave-dwellers who seem remotest from church life who sense that, behind the façade of routine, ritual, and predictability, there exists in some communities a vibrant freedom that expresses itself precisely within the constraining disciplines of asceticism and the common life, in hospitality, and in the exacting demands of mutual service, work, and worship.

From Individual to Person

It is important to know how "to return to oneself" and "to dwell with oneself." These are two expressions that Saint Benedict's biographer uses to describe what his life in the cave was all about. It is surely necessary for anyone to have that sense of oneself if one is to develop inner freedom and an awareness of responsibility.

Notice how those two words go together: *freedom* and *responsibility.* To be truly free is to realize that one is responsible, which means "answerable." This is precisely the difference between being an individual and becoming a person. The very meaning of being a free person is to love, to be committed, to belong, to dedicate one's freedom. The individual will never consecrate himself in this way; he will never commit his freedom, he will never love: until he does, he will never become a person.

One of the illnesses of our contemporary urban cultures is that people are less willing, less able, to live the mystery of human solidarity, to participate and to share. Outside the immediate circle of family and friends, one senses increasingly, across the barriers of anonymity, an isolation stronger than reserve, an introversion bordering almost on the schizoid. People, quite commonly, no longer relate with, or even know, their immediate neighbors.

Within families, not only is the commitment between spouses increasingly problematical, but things so normal as shared entertainments, family holidays, and even meals together are becoming less common and more likely to cause friction and tension. In that context, the atrophy of church life and liturgy can be seen for what it is: another symptom of a much more generalized sickness of our society.

Toward a True Catholicism

The Lord God said, "It is not good that the man to be alone" (Gen 2:18). One could multiply texts from world literature and philosophy affirming the same truth: that no man is an island, that the individual cannot become human by him- or herself. The reciprocity of persons, the centrality of the *I-Thou* relationship can be said to be universal experiences, a fundamental benchmark of what it means to be human. The bond of human solidarity is, however, something even more fundamental than the one-to-one relationships in which we are all engaged. It is at the level of this universal bond that we must situate the great mysteries that touch our shared humanity: original sin, the incarnation, the redemption, and the church.

Different cultures have attempted to explicate this basic relationship in their various ways. For the Greeks, and for their Roman disciple-philosophers, the principle of unity was found in the ideal essence of mankind subsisting in the world of Pure Ideas. For the Jews, as for many peoples, the succession of generations within the people is the essential bond. So it is that Matthew's Gospel starts with a genealogy of Jesus Christ that begins with the patriarch Abraham, to whom the messianic promises had been made, for himself and for all his descendants (Matt 1:1–16). Luke universalizes this ethnic relationship by tracing his genealogy of Jesus right back to "Adam, son of God" (Luke 3:23–38). This is to include every person who ever has been or who ever will be, through the bond of common origin and belonging, within God's work of universal salvation.

Modern literature and philosophy have found their own ways to express the essentially *ecclesial* nature of humanity.[6] Dostoevsky, for instance, sees the relationship between people as more than a passive belonging: it is an active responsibility. This means that, unlike Cain, the murderer who disclaims responsibility, I am obliged to admit that *I am my brother's keeper;* that I am in some mysterious way responsible for my brothers and sisters (Gen 4:9).

In *The Brothers Karamazov,* the dying boy Markel speaks of this bond of responsibility:

> "Everyone of us is responsible for everyone else in every way. And I most of all." Mother could not help smiling at that. She wept and smiled at the same time. "How are you," she said, "most of all responsible for everyone? There are murderers and robbers in the world, and what terrible sin have you committed that you should accuse yourself before everyone else?" "Mother," he said, "you must realise that everyone is really responsible for everyone and everything. I don't know how to explain it to you, but I feel it so strongly that it hurts."[7]

Antoine de Saint-Exupéry has the same intuition in a very different situation. He is a fighter pilot in an air force that has lost its war beyond all hope of recovery. He continues nonetheless for months with pointless and often highly dangerous missions. Why does he do it? Slowly, he comes to understand the ever-widening circles of solidarity and responsibility that impel him to carry on: he is one of a squadron, a pilot in the air force, a member of one of the few units still operational in the French armed forces. He is a Frenchman who must stand firm against tyranny on behalf of all his compatriots. Ultimately and absolutely, he is a human person answerable to and for all others. He owes it, even to his enemies, to fight for what he knows to be right.

> Each individual is responsible for all. Each individual is alone responsible. Each individual is alone respon-

sible for all. For the first time I understand one of the mysteries of that religion which gave birth to the civilization I claim as my own: to bear the sins of men; and each individual bears all the sins of all men.[8]

His own lived experiences brought the Lithuanian-born Jewish philosopher Emmanuel Levinas to reflect deeply on this question of human solidarity. Formed in the crucible of anti-Semitic persecution under the Third Reich, he came to understand that the bond between people is not merely a comfortable I-Thou relationship between familiar and like-minded persons: it is a radical *(pré-originelle)* and inescapable responsibility that preexists between myself and all others, and most especially any person in need with whom I come in contact. Levinas calls this relationship by a surprising name, one that is—as in the case of Saint-Exupéry—very evocative of the Christian mystery: *expiation.*[9]

In a remarkable book, Xavier Le Pichon, Professor of Geodynamics at the Collège de France, draws together the strands of a rich and multifaceted experience, as a brilliant scientist, a man of faith, and as one who has chosen to embrace the mystery of human suffering and handicap by living with his family since 1976 in one of Jean Vanier's *L'Arche* communities. At every level of his knowledge and experience he finds that the helpless, those who suffer, the rejects of society are the prophets whom God sends us. If we welcome these, they become for us a transforming grace, so that a community of love begins to radiate out from this nucleus. The Son of God, by taking our human condition and becoming himself a man of sorrows, has shown us that the only possible answer to evil is still greater love.[10]

The subtitle of Le Pichon's inspired book says it all: *De la Mort à l'Amour*. It is by embracing our humanity at its lowest common denominator, death, that we enter upon the transfiguration of that same human family and its apotheosis, which is love.

We must rethink church, not just in institutional, juridical, organizational, or sociological terms, but at this deepest level of our human solidarity; because that is precisely where the Son of God has come to be *Emmanuel*—God with us, accepting responsibility for us, his brothers and sisters, bearing our sins and our sorrows; with us as our savior and our expiation. Through the mystery of the incarnation, the church is the assembly, the commonwealth of all the redeemed, of *all*.

> For the one who sanctifies and those who are sanctified all have one Father. For this reason Jesus is not ashamed to call them brothers and sisters, saying, "I will proclaim your name to my brothers and sisters, in the midst of the congregation I will praise you."…Since, therefore, the children share flesh and blood, he himself likewise shared the same things, so that through death he might destroy the one who has the power of death, that is the devil, and free those who all their lives were held in slavery by the fear of death. (Heb 2:11–15)

These are the universalist perspectives we must have in mind when we reflect on the church and on our own spiritual growth. It is in and with the church that we share in the commonwealth of Jesus Christ, the Son of God, who assures us of his abiding presence among us: "Remember, I am with you always, to the end of the age" (Matt 28:20). Here we break the bread of God's word and are nourished by the sacraments that are the tangible signs of his enduring presence among us. Most especially in the Eucharist, the paschal meal of the new covenant, God's people are brought together in unity, recognizing Jesus in the breaking of bread (Luke 24:30–31,35).

We know how passionately Jesus prayed for that unity on the night before he died. In that prayer he held together in one embrace the whole of humanity, to which he belongs through his incarnation, and his own union with Father and Holy Spirit in the life of the Blessed Trinity.

> "I ask not only on behalf of these, but also on behalf of those who will believe in me through their word, that they may be all one. As you, Father, are in me and I am in you, may they also be in us, so that the world may believe that you have sent me. The glory that you have given me I have given them, so that they may be one, as we are one, I in them and you in me, that they may become completely one, so that the world may know that you have sent me and have loved them even as you have loved me." (John 17:20–23)

This is Christ's own sublime vision of the church and of its mission. The church is to reflect the glory of Christ, which is the Father's gift to the Son, since before the foundation of the world. In other words, the church is to radiate the beauty of the Blessed Trinity, so that the world may believe.

To accept our solidarity in a sinful humanity and in a very imperfect church is to follow in the footsteps of Christ himself. It is also to allow God to be God, to open ourselves to the way that God has come and continues to come to us, to give precedence to how God seeks us, rather than to how, in our vanity, we might propose to find God.

This is also to open our eyes to how much goodness, generosity, and even heroism there is in ordinary people, how much there is to love and admire where previously—in our arrogance, it may be—we saw only crassness and stupidity. Christ's promise of his enduring presence with his church and the gift he has made us of the Holy Spirit as counselor and protector (John 14:16,26): these are the firm foundations of our confidence and trust—in spite of the worst that human folly can do. Hence Christ's own belief in his church: "When the Advocate comes, whom I will send to you from the Father, the Spirit of truth who comes from the Father, he will testify on my behalf. You also are to testify because you have been with me from the beginning" (John 15:26–27).

The *Pleroma*

The *pleroma* means the fullness, as opposed to the dispersed and fragmented. Saint Paul uses this word to express the mystery of Christ and the church, the reconciliation of all humanity and of the whole universe in Christ.

He is the image of the invisible God,
The firstborn of all creation,
For in him all things in heaven and on earth were
    created....
He himself is before all things
And in him all things hold together,
He is the head of the body, the church.
He is the beginning,

The firstborn from the dead,
So that he might come to have first place in
     everything.
For in him all the *fullness* of God was pleased to
     dwell....(Col 1:15–19)

The individual is called to share this *pleroma* by being part of Christ's body, which is the church. Paul makes this explicit by addressing each one of us directly: "In him the whole fullness of deity dwells bodily, and you have come to fullness in him" (Col 2:9–10).

This perspective is opposed, not only to anything solipsistic or narrowly individualistic in spirituality, but equally to anything elitist, classbound, or in any way exclusivist. This is another of the ambiguities of a purely personal spirituality: it need admit no one except those who affirm me and confirm me in my tastes and prejudices, those whom I find stimulating and congenial. The real church is far less convenient, being recruited from among the riffraff, the poor, and the unclean of city streets and alleyways, the scarecrows of open roads and hedgegrows (Luke 14:21–23).

"There is no longer Jew or Greek, there is no longer slave or free, there is no longer male and female, for all of you are one in Christ Jesus" (Gal 3:28).

The Church's Future

Our confidence is founded on Christ, "who loved the church and gave himself up for her, in order to make her holy by cleansing her with the washing of water by the word, so as to present the church to himself in splendor, without a spot or wrinkle or anything of the kind—yes, so that she may be holy and without blemish" (Eph 5:25–27). Here is that church in the vision of our faith and hope:

> I saw the holy city, the new Jerusalem, coming down out of heaven from God, prepared as a bride adorned for her husband. And I heard a loud voice from the throne saying, "See, the home of God is among mortals. He will dwell with them as their God; they will be his peoples, and God himself will be with them." (Rev 21:2–3)

In the Meantime

In the meantime, brothers and sisters, we wish you happiness; try to grow perfect; help one another. Be united; live in peace, and the God of love and peace will be with you. (2 Cor 13:11)

PART TWO

Vantage Points

To situate the four chapters of this middle part, it will be useful to reread quickly pages x–xi of the introduction.

CHAPTER NINE

One Man's Celibacy

He who is not spiritual in his flesh becomes carnal even in his spirit.

The speaker, Saint Augustine, had some experience in the matter. Paul Evdokimov expresses the same idea in reverse when he quotes Nietzsche, "In true love, the soul encloses the body." Evdokimov adds, "The married as well as the monastic state are two forms of chastity, each one appropriate to its own mode of being." He quotes John Chrysostom, "When husband and wife are united in marriage, they are no longer seen as something earthly, but as the image of God himself." Evdokimov comments, "These words of St. John Chrysostom allow us to see in marriage a living icon of God himself, a *theophany.*"[1]

It is, no doubt, this spiritual bond between the two states of marriage and monasticism that accounts for what seems at first sight a curious fact. From the very beginnings of monasticism, married people, who could easily have consulted their local married clergy, traveled in numbers to the deserts of Egypt, Syria, and Palestine to seek the advice of gnarled old ascetics about the enigmas and trials of married life. Intuitively, they understood the deep connection between the charisms of married and celibate life.

This has probably been better understood in the Eastern Churches, Uniate and Orthodox, than in the Latin Church. "The one who loves," Chrysostom exclaims, "has another self." A true husband does not hesitate to die for his wife. He tells her, "You are more precious than my soul." So it is that Chrysostom can see in every marriage the wedding at Cana and the real presence of Christ, the celibate one, who lays down his life for his bride.[2] "Husbands love your wives, just as Christ loved the church and gave himself up for her" (Eph 5:25). To spiritualize in this way does not mean to disembody; it means to humanize.

"The celibate, like the oppressed, always make music."[3] It is on the basis of the complementarity between these two charisms of married and celibate love—neither of them, we could note, free from a certain oppression—that I presume to make music about a kind of loving and a sort of fruitfulness. This has to be in the nature of a minority report, one made from the ex-centric vantage point of the celibate. But we eccentrics come from families and homes too. Tomaš Špidlík has pointed out the importance of this common ground: "Because marriage is a school of love, its dignity was for Chrysostom a necessary postulate for the demonstration of his thesis on virginity. As an expression of perfect charity, virginity is rooted in the family environment."[4] Having learned and continued to learn so much from loving families who affirm us and support us in our vocation, it would be gratifying if we celibates could share some crumbs of experience and wisdom in return. This is one man's version of it.

Wifeless

Shortly after arriving in Africa for the first time, in 1979, I was emptying rubbish at the monastery dump.[5] Within minutes, two little boys were scavenging among my junk. They emerged triumphant with two shiny tobacco tins, invaluable for storage in a land of insects and humidity. I was instantly ashamed of the opulence that allowed me to jettison what others would scramble for. Shame turned to guilt when I remembered that both tins had served as ashtrays and were still stuffed with the fallout from my self-indulgent lifestyle: cigarette butts and ashes, nicotine-smeared tissues and pipe cleaners, burnt matches and beer tops. I was mortified to think of these children having to scrape my filth off their newfound treasures.

Talking to an African friend some days later, I was bemoaning the absurdity of a European monk purporting to bear witness to gospel poverty among a people whose lifestyle was ten times poorer than his own. My friend smiled and said, "Father, for an African, a man without a wife is the poorest of the poor." I was very surprised by this novel thought. Was it, I wondered, just another example of African male-dominant mentality, or was there something deeper in it?

Some time later I chanced on the Hebrew text of Ecclesiasticus, which, presumably, Jesus would have read. This asserts that "a man without a wife is a tramp and a wanderer" (Sir 36:25). That fits well with mainstream Old Testament thinking: Marriage is good, celibacy is bad, and childlessness is the ultimate disaster. Tramp and wanderer, the poorest of the poor, the man with no wife, the text continued, is one with "no nest, who lodges wherever night overtakes him" (Sir 36:27).

Thinking about these texts led me inevitably to recall what is written of Jesus. As they were going along the road, someone said to him, "I will follow you wherever you go." Jesus said to him, "Foxes have holes and birds of the air have nests, but the Son of man has nowhere to lay his head" (Luke 9:57–58).

In a sense, Jesus is a tramp and a wanderer. A man with no nest, he has nowhere to lay his head. I had always taken these words to refer to the homelessness of Jesus, his itinerant lifestyle, his lack of regular accommodation. In a word, a text about poverty. But read in the context of the Old Testament and of my African guru's precious saying, does not this text also speak powerfully of Jesus' celibacy? He has no nest. This signifies more than the absence of a permanent address. It means that no wife, no children await his return. Jesus has nowhere to lay his head. This says that there is no breast, no shoulder, no lips where he can lay his head, his cheek, his lips. For the first time, after many years as a monk, the celibacy of Jesus actually seemed relevant to my own.

Childless

Jesus commended those who have made themselves eunuchs "for the sake of the kingdom of heaven" (Matt 19:12). If this startles us, it must have struck his hearers as truly shocking. In Jewish society, the eunuch was an outsider, excluded from the priesthood and even from public worship. The later tradition adopted a gentler tone, promising to the God-fearing eunuch "a most desirable portion in the temple of the Lord," which meant in the next life (Wis 3:14; Isa 56:3–5). In *this* life, the eunuch shared the alienation and stigma of the barren woman. To be childless was a disgrace.

In Western culture, where contraception and abortion are taken for granted, it is difficult to hear the pain of Rachel, "Give me children, or I shall die" (Gen 30:1). And what can we make of Jephthah's daughter, who became a wanderer to lament, not that she must die at her own father's hand, but that she should die childless? (Judg 11:34–40).

Paradoxically, today it is often the celibate who can best hear these plaintive accents. That, after all, is where he or she is at. It was the maiden daughters of Israel who both accompanied Jephthah's daughter in her wandering and each year left home to wander again in memory of her tragedy. See how the themes cluster yet again: childlessness, homelessness, wandering.

It was not from within a culture of death, nor even from one so ambiguous about new life as is our own, that Jesus praised those who have made themselves eunuchs for the sake of the kingdom of heaven. It was against the backdrop of the marriage feast of Cana, where he gave the first of his signs (John 2:11), that Jesus himself embarked upon his own radical lifestyle as a "eunuch" and invited "anyone who can" to follow him in this paradox. He promised a hundredfold, and eternal life, to those who would accept that challenge, which, humanly speaking, must have a very high risk factor for failure.

In trying to understand my own celibacy, I had always avoided this "eunuch" text in Matthew's Gospel, finding it embarrassing and distasteful. Celibate or not, who likes to be called a eunuch? Each time I encountered it, I wished that Jesus had chosen some softer, euphemistic word—as indeed many translators do. Only after many years did I discover that I had been misreading the text, or rather half-reading it, because it does not stop there.

Having reported Jesus' saying about those who have made themselves eunuchs for the sake of the kingdom of heaven, Matthew continues immediately:

> Then little children were being brought to him in order that he might lay his hands on them and pray. The disciples spoke sternly to those who brought them; but Jesus said, "Let the little children come to me, and do not stop them; for it is to such as these that the kingdom of heaven belongs." And he laid his hands on them and went on his way. (Matt 19:13)

Isaiah had promised to the barren and desolate woman even more children than the wedded wife (Isa 54:1), and to the eunuch, "better than sons and daughters" (Isa 56:5). Here Jesus, himself a eunuch for the sake of the kingdom, comes into his inheritance. These children of the kingdom, to whom the kingdom of heaven belongs, are *his* children, as are all those who will welcome the kingdom with childlike simplicity (Mark 10:15). That is why the children must not be stopped from coming to Jesus. There is surely an intended continuity between the evocation of the childlessness of Jesus for the kingdom and the right of access to Jesus for the children of that same kingdom.

Saint Paul quotes the Isaiah text just referred to, about the children born to the barren and desolate woman, when he speaks of the children born through the Spirit (Gal

4:26–31). For him, Jesus is the second Adam, father of a whole new humanity, and it is he who gives life in the Spirit (1 Cor 15:45). Jesus, poor, homeless, without wife or children, has become spouse of the church (Eph 5:23–32) and father of the children of the kingdom. The scriptural and patristic texts speaking of the fatherhood of Jesus are surprisingly numerous, especially when one considers that the main emphasis of orthodoxy in the early church had to be on Christ's relationship as *Son* to the Father.

Whether or not we shall one day have married clergy in the Latin Church again, it seems certain that the charism of celibacy in the pattern of Christ will continue to enrich the church, East and West. Many in the active ministry, as also those in religious life, and many private individuals, some of them after happy married lives, will be called to share in the mystery of Christ's celibate love and fruitfulness.

On the other hand, in the light of all that the church has experienced and learned in recent years—some of it very painfully—it does seem essential that nobody should be admitted to a permanent commitment to celibacy without a clear discernment that he or she has received this charism. It cannot be assumed that the free gifts of the Spirit will flow in accordance with the requirements of particular regimes of clerical organization and discipline. What is done or not done in this area will have serious consequences both in relation to the number and to the suitability of candidates presenting themselves for the priesthood in the future.

Consecrated celibacy is not just a question of being more available for works of ministry—many celibates will have no identifiable ministry at all—nor is their fruitfulness a matter of being able to count the heads of those to whom they have become father in Christ Jesus through the gospel

(1 Cor 4:15). Jesus himself in his lifetime met and knew an infinitesimally small number of the children that God had given him (Heb 2:13). I believe that this is so also for those who have received the charism of celibate love and fruitfulness.

Celibates, eunuchs, tramps, wanderers for Christ and for the kingdom, rejoice!

CHAPTER TEN

The Little Black Girl in Search of God

A Celebration of a Living Spirituality

African children have beautiful teeth.[1] Everybody knows that. Teeth dazzling, in perfect alignment; and they are strong. Your host's son may set *your* teeth on edge by opening beer bottles with *his*. These children smile a lot. It seems reasonable to suppose some correlation between smiles, nice teeth, and psychological, even spiritual, well-being.

Spiritual? Yes, I think so. We accept the psychosomatic, the interaction of mind and body. Why not the pneumasomatic as well, the epiphany of the Spirit in the forms and language of the body? Was it not Jung who said that by the age of forty, every man has the face he deserves? It was certainly he who recorded the physiognomic observations of an Indian chief in New Mexico:

See how cruel the whites look. Their lips are thin, their noses sharp, their faces furrowed and distorted....Their eyes have a staring expression; they are always seeking something; what are they seeking? The whites always want something; they are always uneasy and restless....We do not understand them. We think that they are mad.[2]

Having been fortunate, apparently, to meet nicer black children than the New Mexican chief met white adults, I should like to table some observations of my own. These will not stray far from the physical base, things seen and heard, simple, as are the things of childhood, but not insignificant. What is humanly rich is Spirit filled and never trivial.

So why do African children have beautiful teeth? There are, no doubt, genetic reasons; and plenty of sunshine does make for good bones, but diet too is a principal factor. Low sugar, no additives, no hormones or cowboy chemicals, no junk food to poison the system and rot out the teeth. Besides, these children rarely eat between meals and, though adequately nourished, do not often eat to their hunger. Fasting, in the sense of eating no more than one needs, is the everyday experience of almost any African child. This, as ascetics of all traditions have forever known, is good for the body, good for the mind and the spirit, and good too for the teeth. It is on record that the Great Saint Anthony, after eighty years of asceticism in the desert, at the age of 105, still had all his teeth.

We should remember, too, that African teenagers in great majority do not smoke, drink alcohol, or take drugs. Quite simply, they are unpolluted. This comprehensive freedom from toxicity, with the self-discipline and temperance it implies, goes deeper than the purely physical. The smiling face and flashing teeth attest an inner freedom and a self-respect that many youngsters in the Western world have lost or never had.

It is not just teeth, of course; it is a whole way of inhabiting a body, a poetry of poise and movement, a rhythm of dancers, drummers, and effortless carriers of everything on the head. A veteran Olympic medallist raised protests for suggesting that young blacks are more gifted naturally for athletics than others. Some said that this was racism, and racism going in an unfamiliar direction. Well, just watch African children at play—skimming the earth, shimmering through the air like silver porpoises in and over the water. No equipment, no coach, no commercialism, no fulsome praise for the clever little darlings. It is all pure fun, and second nature. That too gives glory to God and is very good for the soul.

Liturgy is of its nature pneumasomatic. The spirit dances, sings, welcomes, processes, proclaims, offers, receives, rejoices, and mourns. That is the theory. In Africa it is the reality, as it can be only where people rejoice with Christ to say, "You gave me a body....Here I am!" (Heb 10:5). It is sad to be in churches where there are too few bodies, and nobody seems very happy inside the ones that are there.

Dress, too, for the liturgy of life. In conditions where water is scarce, and where climate, housing, and insects go hard on fabrics, how do people manage to be always immaculate? Their clothes are homemade or the work of village tailors. A kaleidoscope of colors that never seem to clash, worn with hieratic elegance. Besides, these are *real* clothes that express the personalities of their wearers, not the anonymous gear that seems to have invaded the rest of the planet.

I know an outstation of a poverty-stricken country parish in Nigeria where the people are determined to provide six sets of mass-servers' outfits, each with five cassocks, one in each of the liturgical colors: a total of thirty garments. It is crazy, of course, and the people can ill afford it. But that is what Judas said about the woman in the gospel with the jar of precious ointment. In Africa, clothes are sacramental, and there are priorities.

Strong bonds of family affection and the still-close ties of village society make for children who are open and self-confident. At the same time, there is a strong sense of hierarchy. Children, teenagers, even adults show marked respect, for parents, for elders, and traditional rulers. This respect manifests itself in speech, but also in an expressive and captivating body language. Girls curtsy gracefully, boys make solemn bows of head and shoulders. In some tribes, these reverences come nearer to genuflection and prostration.

One is never casual. In giving or receiving even a nondescript object like a *biro*, a young person will hold out both hands in an almost liturgical gesture. To accept a gift, a boy may drop down on one knee, like a knight to his dubbing. Even more alarming for the newcomer is the unsolicited valet service. At any point in conversation an ebony hand may dart out to pick insects, vegetation, or debris off one's face, beard, hair, or clothes. No commentary or explanation is offered, and all these civilities are rendered spontaneously, without the smallest trace of awkwardness or servility.

"Manners maketh the man," and "Grace builds on nature." Two clichés, of course, but they both happen to be true. Such banalities as good manners play an important role in spirituality. A sister asked me once, "Have you noticed that people do to other people what they do to their food?" Interesting, don't you think?

In African society, overt flirtation between boys and girls is strictly taboo. It is perfectly normal, however, to see teenage boys or young men holding hands. Any suggestion that this could have sexual overtones would be received with open-mouthed astonishment. Young Africans are generally disgusted by the sexual crassness of much Western cinema and publishing. There is a common myth in the West that blacks are highly sexed. They are hardly deficient in that respect, but the catastrophic incidence of AIDS and venereal diseases in some areas can be attributed to many factors besides depravity and promiscuity.

Whatever their sexual exploits, African boys and girls are most notably different from many of their Western contemporaries in their unshaken belief in the family, their hope to marry some day, and their ardent desire to be blessed with children. These values do seem increasingly threatened in the Northern Hemisphere, where many young people seem increasingly preoccupied with individual fulfilment, not to say gratification, to the point of eschewing marriage and childbearing altogether. I am not talking about responsible family planning; I am talking about no children at all, or at least not until all other needs and wants are satisfied. The result is whole nations rapidly becoming sad, vast, fortified colonies of the elderly, bereft of young people—yet still determined to keep the fertile immigrants out. Perhaps the most fundamental question about any civilization or in any spirituality is, What do people hope for?

Another important difference is that when young Africans feel guilty, they do not immediately assume that this is a neurosis but are disposed to believe that they have probably done something wrong. Neither would it be correct to attribute their attitude to a puritanical colonial Christian upbringing that can be supposed to have contaminated the joyful springs of native African spontaneity, especially in the area of sexuality. The myth of the "noble savage," and of the good times that he had, dies hard. Traditional African society, as also the influential Islamic culture, are in fact rigorous in most areas of morality and indeed disapprove of churches that they perceive as dispensing facile forgiveness for serious infringements.

Transcending all purely moral questions is the massive reality of African spirituality. Christian, Moslem, traditional believers: all live in the presence of *a cloud of witnesses* (Heb 12:1): ancestors, good and evil spirits, God himself. There is fear and superstition—but you do not have to go to Africa for that—there is also a deep core of trust and hope. In the context of religious conversion or to follow a vocation, a young person will accept great hardship and will not be deterred by intimidating and even violent opposition. They believe, they care, and they go for it.

In too many African countries, corruption and malpractice of every kind have reached such proportions that it is no longer a question of cheating the system: cheating *is* the system. Children will have learned that bitter lesson long before leaving school. It is hateful to see them sucked inexorably into this soul-destroying miasma. And yet, Africa is not just a bubbling cauldron of bribery and corruption, nor yet one vast refugee camp, nor a continent inhabited by skeletons and begging bowls. Africa is rich in things that matter. Not least of these is a vibrant and youthful spirituality.

CHAPTER ELEVEN

Monastic Spirituality

It is said that the Rule of Saint Benedict has been translated more often than any other book except the Bible.[1] There are at least a dozen English versions currently in circulation, and scores of others in many languages. The secondary literature, too, is enormous, ranging from commentaries, through monographs on literary, historical, and spiritual aspects of the rule, to books, articles, tapes, and CDs presenting monastic life in a great variety of different perspectives: popular piety, therapy, alternative lifestyle, neoromanticism, gnosticism for the elite, basic Christianity for everyone, school of prayer, mystic path—the list is extensive. Most monasteries have their own literature as well, presenting themselves to the many enthusiastic pilgrims and sightseers who arrive. Finally, and increasingly, there are comparative studies about Eastern and Western, Christian and non-Christian forms of monasticism, and specifically about the possibility and problems of implanting Benedictine and Cistercian life in Southern Hemisphere cultures.

Significant contributions are being made in this whole area by people who are neither monks nor nuns[2] nor, in some cases, Christians or even believers. Culturally, their interest is understandable, because monasticism did play an important role in the emergence of Western civilization and is still one of the strongest contact points between Western and Asiatic cultures. What is less obvious is why so many people, scholars and simple folk alike, still find Benedict's wisdom and way of life relevant and enriching, in an era when so much else that seemed valuable and good has been left behind.

Benedict himself would be the first to express surprise, were he to return today, fifteen hundred years after his death. He would be astonished to learn that he had founded a great religious order that has lasted until the present time, and even more astounded to hear that he is regarded as one of the patrons of Europe. He would probably need explanations about what a religious order is and parameters to the political and social concept of Europe. Not much of all that has ensued over the centuries in his name would seem to have featured on Benedict's original agenda. He did not plan things that way. His simple life sowed a seed: God gave the growth and the harvest.

This seems characteristic of Benedictine life even today. Its essential witness and apostolate are no more specific or proactive than the overriding principle that Benedict took from scripture and enshrined in his rule "that in all things God may be glorified."[3] The emphasis is not on what a person or a community can achieve for the church and society, but on whether they are striving for that *purity of heart* in God's service without which all achievement is ultimately self-serving.

Benedict was born about AD 480 at Nursia, northeast of Rome, and never strayed more than a few days' journey from the place of his birth. He was moderately well educated up to the age of sixteen or seventeen, when he fled from the worldly or worse atmosphere of student life in Rome, still "wisely unlearned," as his biographer says. Settling in a cave in the hill country of Subiaco, he lived as a hermit until early manhood. Then, coaxed from his solitude by some neighboring monks who thought he might make a good abbot, he eventually founded twelve monasteries.

If two attempts on his life are anything to go by, Benedict was hardly a great abbot at that time. Too ardent perhaps, too idealistic, he was certainly inexperienced and probably intolerant. His famous *Rule for Monks,* written some forty years later at Monte Cassino, bears all the signs of holy wisdom, gentle patience, and a loving understanding of human nature, acquired the hard way, by experience, through many trials, and with not a few errors along the way.

Virtually everything we know about Benedict is contained in that rule or in the charming life of the saint attributed to Pope Saint Gregory the Great. There are no spectacular achievements recorded in either document, unless it be some nicely appropriate miracles, which historians would probably discount, or that least dramatic of miracles, which they might not even notice at all: tiny communities of stable, harmonious, orderly, hospitable, and God-centered life sprouting amid the rubble of a ransacked and ruined empire.

If men and women today are still turning to communities where *Peace, work and pray,* and *Prefer nothing to Christ* are the familiar watchwords, it is surely not in search of sophisticated ideas or esoteric wisdom. They are attracted by a simple art of spiritual living and by the slow-release miracle of God's fidelity and love in the long endurance of daily life. That is what this whole book is about.

Searching for God

A priest coming to join Benedict's monastery was greeted with the words, "Friend, why have you come?" (RB 60:3). Is it coincidence that this is what Jesus said to Judas, who had just arrived to betray him with a kiss? (Matt 26:50).

Benedictine novices are encouraged to ask themselves frequently, not just during their novitiate but throughout their monastic life, "Why did I come here?" There is a danger that they might forget; and the first degree of humility, Benedict tells us, is "to keep the fear of God always before one's eyes, and to shun all forgetfulness" (RB 7:10).

People come to monasteries for all sorts of reasons. Sometimes these reasons are patently inappropriate: to evade conscription into the army or detection by the police, to avoid starvation, to escape domestic unhappiness or professional or moral failure, to flee emotionally or psychologically unmanageable situations. Some people join monasteries to get away from other people—maybe parents or persons of the opposite sex, or just as many people as possible. Others just want security, predictability, safe routines, regular feeding, health care, and accommodation, without too much bother.

There are also ambivalent motivations. An interest in liturgy, in sacred music, art, scholarship, or some apostolate or activity associated with the particular monastery chosen. One may come, attracted by a charismatic abbot or some other figure within the community whom one perceives as a viable guru or *anam cara*.

Most monastic vocations are buttressed by one or several secondary motivations, some of them quite superficial. The Holy Spirit can use these fads and favorites like booster rockets to get a neophyte "into orbit," but none of them has sufficient impetus for the journey still out ahead. Sooner or later, all must burn out and fall away. The vital question then is, What, if anything, is left?

Saint Benedict is credited with the invention of novitiates and novice masters, at least in the sense of designated persons and places, and a prescribed program of twelve months' duration. The novitiate was a time of formation and acclimatization to the strange world of monastic living. More essentially, in Benedict's mind, it was a process of testing and investigation. This had nothing to do with those regimes of eccentric commands, artificial humiliations, and false accusations that became fashionable in later, more rococo times. Quite to the contrary, the essential business of Benedict's novitiate was always, and should still be, reality and truth.

> A senior chosen for his skill in winning souls should be appointed to look after (the novices) with careful attention. His concern must be to find out whether the novice truly seeks God. (RB 58:6)

There is only *one* necessary and sufficient reason to be or stay in a monastery: that is the conviction that this is where God wants me to be, to seek and to find him. Whether or not *I* want it, in the sense of finding life easy and the company congenial, is not the essential issue. Besides, as in marriage and in all walks of life, there are good times and bad times. The monk must be "ambidextrous," as Cassian says, able to turn bad times and good to spiritual advantage (Conf. 6). His fundamental sense of vocation must be sufficiently deep and focussed to survive both. Monasteries are not spiritual comfort zones. They are "schools of the Lord's service" (Prol. 45).

Fundamental Perspectives

Reverential awe, it has been said, is the central spiritual value of Benedict's Rule. The monastery is the household of God in whose presence the monk is living at every moment and wherever he may be, "at the work of God, in the oratory, in the monastery, in the garden, on the road, in a field, or anywhere else, whether he is sitting, walking or standing" (RB 7:63).

It is this fundamental reality of God's presence that inspires and motivates the profound sentiments of attentiveness, obedience, humility, reverence, and love that should characterize every aspect of monastic life. Reverential awe is not servile fear. On the contrary, Benedict promises that, by the Holy Spirit's action, all that we initially perform with dread, we will "soon" begin to observe through "the perfect love of God which casts out fear (1 John 4:18), without effort, as though naturally, from habit, no longer out of fear of hell, but out of love for Christ, good habit, and delight in virtue" (RB 7:67–70).

Three times Benedict tells us that we should "prefer nothing to the love of Christ" (RB 4:21; 5:2; 72:11). Christ is the true king for whom we fight (Prol. 3), whom we follow in hardship (Prol. 50; 4:10) and to glory (Prol. 7). It is Christ whom we reverence and serve in our superiors and communities, in guests, the poor, pilgrims, and "above and before all else, in the sick who must be truly served as Christ, for he said 'I was sick and you visited me' and 'what you did for one of these least brothers you did for me'" (RB 36:1–3). To Christ also we turn in times of temptation, dashing our evil thoughts against "the rock which is Christ" (Prol. 28; 4:50).

If we seek God and serve Christ in all these ways, it is because it is he who seeks us first.

Seeking his workman in a multitude of people, the Lord calls out, "Is there anyone here who yearns for life and desires to see good days?" If you hear this and your answer is "I do," God then directs these words to you, "If you desire true and eternal life, keep your tongue free from vicious talk and your lips from all deceit; turn away from evil and do good; seek peace and pursue it. Once you have done this, my eyes will be upon you and my ears will listen for your prayers; and even before you ask me, I will say to you: Here I am." What, dear brothers, is more delightful than this voice of the Lord calling to us? See how the Lord in his love shows us the way of life. Clothed then with faith and the performance of good works, let us set out on this way, with the Gospel for our guide, that we may deserve to see him who has called us to his kingdom. (Prol. 14–21)

The Ladder of Humility

Benedict wishes his disciple's life and action to be founded on the truth of the relationship between God and ourselves. Humility is the truthful expression of that relationship. The word *humilitas* comes from *humus,* the good earth. The humble person has his feet on the ground. He lives with reality, the reality of God's utter love as the source of everything that is good, and the truth also of our own sinfulness.

Place your hope in God alone. If you notice something good in yourself, give credit to God, not to yourself, but be certain that the evil you commit is always your own and yours to acknowledge. (RB 4:41–43)

Chapter 7 of the rule describes the *ladder of humility* that the monk must climb in order to become grounded in truth and so find God. This ladder has twelve rungs. Here they are in résumé:

1. To fear God
2. Not to love one's own will
3. To obey one's superior, for the love of God
4. To endure hard and even unjust treatment with courage and patience
5. To acknowledge one's own faults
6. To be content with shabby, even menial conditions, and not to feel that we deserve better
7. To thank God that our self-importance and pride have been deflated
8. To follow the example of our elders rather than our own self-will
9. To measure our words
10. Not to be shallow and facetious
11. To be gentle, serious, modest, and reasonable in our words
12. And in our whole demeanor

These are unusual prescriptions in a culture where self-esteem and personal promotion are greatly prized. Where, we wonder, could such a program leave us vis-à-vis confreres who might take it less seriously than ourselves? Turning the other cheek is only easy when everybody else is doing it as well. And sometimes monasteries are not like that.

But the ladder of humility is less about how to live with each other than about how to live together in the presence of God. To the extent that we remember this context, the steps of humility begin to make sense. To the extent that we exclude God from our tunnel-vision view of human relations, we remain prey to anger, envy, pride, and a whole range of vengeful and malicious thoughts about those around us.

What the ladder of humility does is to confront us with the real object of our anger and resentment: God himself. There is an old monastic joke—such things do exist—that goes as follows:

> *Question:* Why does Saint Benedict say that the abbot takes the place of Christ in the monastery?

> *Answer:* Because he is the one that we crucify.

Abbots do have a hard time. Monks, like the rest of us, tend to vent their frustrations and insecurities on each other, but especially on their abbots. In Freudian terms, we could see this as a case of Oedipal conflict. An abbot, as the very name suggests, is a *father figure* and as likely a focus for resentment as for reverence.

Freud argues from love and hatred for the human father to religion, as an obsessive neurosis centered on the mental projection we call God. Benedict understands things exactly the other way around. We vent our anger with God and his will on other people, and especially on those who represent his authority. This conflict goes to the heart of the spiritual life, and abbots, or spouses, or whoever, gets crucified in the process.

It is in this context that we can understand Benedict's repeated and severe condemnations of what he calls "murmuring." This has nothing to do with dislike for complaints or criticism. He is perfectly open to both, expressed in the right way and at the right time. Murmuring, in Benedict's view, is a quite different exercise: underhanded, corrosive, and highly dangerous in community because it undermines the faith-trust relationship between the brethren and God himself. Murmuring is cowardly, not so much because it is done behind people's backs, which it nearly always is, but because we make other people whipping boys for our own failures in obedience and trust.

Christ had no complaints about his judges and executioners. They are to be forgiven because "they do not know what they are doing" (Luke 23:34). But what exactly did he mean when he told Pilate, "You would have no power over me if it had not been given you from above; that is why the one who handed me over to you has the greater responsibility" (John 19:11)? Is he merely blaming Judas and the Jewish authorities? And when he cried out on the cross, "My God, my God, why have you forsaken me?" (Matt 27:46), is he simply reciting his psalter? We know that, quite apart from the grubby political and financial calculations of Judas and Caiaphas, there is a much more radical drama being fought out, a potential clash of wills between Jesus and the Father about his fate, a clash that can only be resolved by *kenosis*, self-emptying, the free and loving submission of the Son to his Father's will (Matt 26:39ff).

Saint Benedict defines monastic life in terms of this paschal experience of Christ. "Persevering in his teaching in the monastery until death, we shall share by patience in the sufferings of Christ that we may deserve to share also in his kingdom" (Prol. 50). The ladder of humility helps us to recognize the real issues in our spiritual life, how much anger, pride, and resentment smoulder in our hearts, how pitiless and unloving we can be with those around us and, behind all that and largely unacknowledged, how little we trust God and how ill disposed we are to accept his will, which is always the expression of his boundless love.

The steps of humility are not a checklist of unpleasant things we have to do to ourselves in order to arrive at some notional perfection. They are, rather, a phenomenology of God's creative action within us. Benedict is describing how grace transforms us into people who, accepting ever more willingly what God is doing in our lives, become progressively more aware of who we really are. This self-knowledge is the basis of true peace and personal integration. It is a wonderful grace to be able to watch and assent to the miracle of our own creation.

"All this the Lord will by the Holy Spirit graciously show forth [demonstrare], in his workman now cleansed of vices and sins" (RB 7:70). We have in this demonstration of the Holy Spirit not only a mirror for the purest form of self-love, but also the foundation for a theology of monastic witness. This will never be a matter of putting on a show of superiority or holiness. Nothing could be more obnoxious than that, and Benedict warns us against it (RB 4:62). But a monastic community, and each member of it, can be and should be witnesses to the ongoing slow-release miracle of God's creative love. The flowering of that love comes when, in death, we can joyfully assent to the promise of God's gift of new and everlasting Christ-life in us. "Here am I, the servant of the Lord; let it be with me according to your word" (Luke 1:38).[4]

CHAPTER TWELVE

Signs of the Seeker

In the closing lines of the previous chapter, we anticipated the happy ending to our whole lives. We must now go back to the beginning. Having asked the novice master to investigate whether the novice truly seeks God, Benedict goes on to explain what areas need scrutiny in order to arrive at a reliable answer to that question: Is he zealous for *the Work of God,* for *Obedience,* and for *Trials*? Clearly believing that each of these facets of monastic life is going to be difficult and to test the candidate's mettle, he adds with characteristic forthrightness that "the novice should be clearly told all the hardships and difficulties through which we journey to God" (RB 58:7–8), so that he or she will fully realize what they are getting into (RB 58:12).

The Work of God

What does it mean? In pre-Benedictine monastic tradition, the expression "work of God" *(Opus Dei)* meant anything and everything done in God's service. Benedict, who uses the expression sixteen times, gives it a much sharper focus. The work of God means the community prayer of the monastic family. What is required is a faithful commitment to the worship of God within and together with the worshiping community of God's household, the *domus Dei.* For monks and nuns, this will be their monastic community. For laypeople, if the opportunity offers, it may be an association with a community, a less formalized group, their own families, and most essentially, their parish church.

The monks of Egypt laid more stress on continuous personal prayer than on communal worship. Benedict's few years as a teenaged hermit living in his cave seem to reach back to that venerable tradition. His biographer depicts, with surprising equanimity, a life in which community worship, sacramental piety, and even ecclesial adherence played little if any part. It is indeed remarkable that a saint popularly believed to have founded an order of dedicated liturgists could have gone so "low church" at one point as not even to know when it was Easter Sunday. Even today nonpractice does not come any worse than that.

The mature Benedict of the Rule says categorically, "Let nothing be put before the Work of God" (RB 43:3). This is in no way a plea for the sort of ornate and elaborate liturgy sometimes associated with Benedictines in later centuries. Neither does it mean that he had any explicit sense of the monastic liturgy as the "official prayer of the church." It is nevertheless a firm assertion of the central importance of community worship in Christian life. This intuition remains as perhaps the most significant witness of monks to the church and to the world.

> We believe that the divine presence is everywhere and that "in every place the eyes of the Lord are watching the good and the wicked" (Prov. 15:3). But beyond the least doubt we should believe this to be especially true when we celebrate the divine office.

We must always remember, therefore, what the Prophet says: "Serve the Lord with fear" (Ps 2:11), and again, "Sing praise wisely" (Ps 47:8); and, "In the presence of the angels I will sing to you" (Ps 138:1). Let us consider, then, how we ought to behave in the presence of God and his angels, and let us stand to sing the psalms in such a way that our minds are in harmony with our voices. (RB 19 passim)

This spirit of reverence permeates Benedict's attitude to every aspect of the liturgy. So it is that, at the singing of the doxology, "all rise from their seats in honour and reverence for the Holy Trinity" (RB 9:7), and "stand with respect and awe" when the gospel is proclaimed (RB11:9). Some people feel that the size and fervor of Sunday congregations might increase if there were more emphasis on reverence and less on human inventiveness. The two are surely not incompatible.

Toward the end of his life, Benedict had a vision in which he saw the whole of creation as if contained in a ball of light. He understood how God's presence and love are everywhere. So, too, our love and worship should encounter God's goodness everywhere. This is the secret of the profound respect for each person that Benedict constantly urges, but also for his insistence that even the humblest *things* should be treated with reverence. So the monk must "look upon all the utensils and goods of the monastery as sacred vessels of the altar, aware that nothing should be neglected" (RB 31:10), and whoever fails to keep the things belonging to the monastery clean or treats them carelessly should be reproved (RB 32:4). This is also why monks must "look to the father of the monastery for all their needs....All things should be the common possession of all, as it is written (Acts 4:32), so that no one presumes to call anything his own" (RB 33:5–6).

We are not individual owners, but brothers and sisters who jointly steward and share the wonders of God's creation. These intuitions are richer and more meaningful than ever today, at a time when concern for the environment and for our common birthright has reached global dimensions. Today "preferring nothing to the work of God" means circling the entire planet with our care and reverence.

Personal Prayer

First-time readers of Benedict's Rule are disappointed to find so little about personal prayer and nothing at all about contemplation or mysticism.[1] There is no mention of stages or degrees of prayer, no techniques are suggested for meditation, nor is there any advice about how to cope with dryness or distractions. Benedict is at the furthest remove from envisaging prayer as a neo-gnostic delight for initiates or a well-crafted aesthetically pleasing experience for spiritual gourmets.

Benedict is very sensitive to the differences between people and how uniquely the Spirit acts in each individual soul. If he hesitates to legislate for other people's eating and drinking (RB 40:1–2), how much more reticent will he be about quantifying or measuring their personal prayer. Chapter 20, "On Reverence in Prayer," is a model of this discretion. Benedict stresses humility and pure devotion. He continues, "Let us realise that we shall be heard not in much speaking, but in purity of heart and in compunction and tears." His conclusion is equally direct: "And that is why prayer should be brief and pure, unless it be prolonged by an inspiration of divine grace."

Benedict repeats frequently throughout the rule his advice that prayer should be simple and heartfelt. "If at other times he wishes to pray more secretly by himself, let him simply go in to the oratory and pray, not with a loud voice but with tears and an attentive heart" (RB 52:4). Prayer with tears is a recurring theme (RB 4:57; 49:4). The emphasis is never on methods or techniques, but always on sincerity, attentiveness, spontaneity, and quality rather than quantity.

We have to interpret what Benedict says about prayer against the background of a whole monastic tradition that he inherited from the earliest times. Two fundamental themes in that spirituality are *purity of heart* and *lectio divina*.

Purity of Heart

We have already touched on this topic in the chapters on conversion. The immediate goal of monastic life is to achieve, through asceticism and in combat against evil thoughts, *purity of heart*. This means progressively freeing oneself, by God's grace, from the tyranny of those evil thoughts, feelings, and fantasies that alienate us from God, from each other, from our true selves, and from reality. To the extent that the monk advances in this healing process, he lives more and more permanently in God's presence, with the truth about himself and about the whole of creation. This is, in effect, to live in continuous prayer. Benedict's Rule is, in fact, a phenomenology of this growth in the interior life. It is how he teaches prayer, and it is worth a thousand manuals.

Lectio Divina

Benedict's monks spent up to three hours a day in the slow prayerful reading of scripture. "Reading, meditation, prayer, contemplation. This is the ladder of monks by which they are lifted up from earth to heaven."[2]

This reading in depth is not so much study as "a means of descending to the level of the heart and of finding God."[3] It is the traditional and peculiarly monastic form of prayer.

Obedience

Monastic life is not servitude: it is the willing service of free people. The monastery is not a penitentiary: it is the *domus Dei,* the house of God, and the inhabitants are God's household. Accordingly, Benedict always looks beyond mere compliance with rules and regulations to the inner dispositions of the heart. I have mentioned already how, hearing that Martin the Hermit had chained himself to a rock in his cave so that he could no longer change his mind about monastic life, Benedict sent him an urgent message that the love of Christ alone should bind us rather than iron chains. Could that have an application in family life?

The Latin word *oboedire,* "to obey," is cognate to the word *obaudire,* "to listen." The first word of Benedict's Rule is *Listen!* The monk is, or should be, a listener. Attentive to the signs of the times, he listens for the word of God in the scriptures, in the voice of his abbot, in the tradition and teaching of the church and of the fathers, in the words and needs of his confreres, and of all with whom he comes in contact, especially the poor and the sick.

The monastic tradition has always recognized self-will as the major obstacle, not only to good community relationships but also to friendship with God himself. It is clear, therefore, how the notions of humility and obedience are virtually interchangeable. Neither has anything whatsoever to do with servility or abjectness. Both require a good sense of oneself and an openness to real relationships.

Chapter 72, "On the Good Zeal Which Monks Should Have," is a beautiful summary of Saint Benedict's wise teaching on obedience.

> Just as there is a wicked zeal of bitterness which sep-arates from God and leads to hell, so there is a good zeal which separates from evil and leads to God and everlasting life. This, then, is the good zeal which monks must foster with fervent love: "They should each try to be the first to show respect to the other" (Rom 12:10), supporting with the greatest patience one another's weaknesses of body or behavior, and earnestly competing in obedience to one another. No one is to pursue what he judges better for himself, but instead what he judges better for someone else. To their fellow monks they show the pure love of brothers; to God loving fear; to their abbot sincere and humble love. Let them prefer nothing whatever to Christ, and may he bring us all together to ever-lasting life.

Benedict's abbot is given very wide authority in the rule, authority so wide that canon law and the constitutions of the various Benedictine congregations have seen fit to curtail it, notably in financial matters. But if the abbot's powers are extensive, they come with prodigal warnings. Several times he is reminded that he will answer to God for every one of his decisions, that he must always act with justice, and indeed set mercy above justice. He must seek profit for the monks, not preeminence for himself, and strive to be loved rather than feared. He must be discerning and moderate, bearing in mind the discretion of holy Jacob, who said, "If I drive my flocks too hard, they will all die in a single day" (Gen 33:13). Therefore, drawing on this and other examples of discretion, the mother of virtues, he must so arrange everything that the strong have something to yearn for and the weak nothing to run away from. (RB 64 passim)

Benedict lays down that whenever anything important is to be done in the monastery, the whole community is to be called together, fully briefed on the issues, and asked for their advice. He particularly stresses that *everybody* should be called to counsel. "The reason why we have said all should be called for counsel is that the Lord often reveals what is better to the younger" (RB 3:3). Even in lesser matters, the abbot should seek advice. Benedict quotes the Book of Wisdom: "Do everything with counsel and you will not be sorry afterwards" (Sir 32:24).

The abbot is also told all the things he must *not* be: "Excitable, anxious, extreme, obstinate, jealous or over-suspicious"—and Benedict adds the excellent reason, "Such a man is never at rest" (RB 64:16).

From these remarks it should be evident that, if the abbot is the most powerful person in the monastery, he must also be the most obedient and the one who listens most. Benedict spells it out:

He must know what a difficult and demanding burden he has undertaken: directing souls and serving a variety of temperaments, coaxing some, reproving others, encouraging others again. He must so accommodate and adapt himself to each one's character and intelligence that he will not only suffer no loss in the flock entrusted to his care, but rejoice in the increase of a good flock. (RB 2:31–32)

Unlike some of his predecessors, Benedict is careful not to treat his monks as children. He did, however, have young people in his communities, and older ones who sometimes behaved like children. Parents will find many good things in his rule about how to give the young both the security of knowing where they stand and the reassurance that they are truly valued and loved. Benedict says twice that "the young should *respect* their elders, and the elders should *love* their juniors." Which group gets the more demanding assignment?

Trials

The word used for "trials" is *opprobria*. This could mean insults or contemptuous treatment. Such things can happen in monasteries as elsewhere, but they are not inherent to the monastic way of life. Benedict seems to be referring more to the humble and unpleasant tasks that need to be done in any household, and such as were usually left to slaves in the ancient world. More generally, he has in mind how a person reacts in situations where his pride or his sense of his own dignity, precedence, or competence is punctured or ignored. One does tend to show one's true colors when the bubble of conceit is pricked in these revealing little episodes. Not the least telling aspect of such apparent trivialities is the extent to which they can irk and upset us. Benedict, heir to the wisdom of the desert, has a keen eye for the pettiness that says embarrassingly loud what we are really seeking in life.

If we seem to end on an anticlimax, this too is in fidelity to the spirit of Benedict. Monastic spirituality is for ordinary people with boring lives. It will disappoint those in search of beautiful and intriguing experiences. The exodus from Egypt to the Promised Land leads across the wilderness. The desert is monotonous and the haunt of demons: it also symbolizes in its utter vastness "the infinity of God's love" (Evagrius).

PART THREE

Points of Arrival

CHAPTER THIRTEEN

Has Death a Meaning?

Death as Affirmation

There are deaths that speak for themselves, that affirm their meaning without words. When the centurion, who was standing in front of him, saw how Jesus had died, he exclaimed, "Truly this man was God's Son!" (Mark 15:39).

The Greek word *martur,* from which our word *martyr* derives, has really nothing to do with death: it means "one who affirms" or "bears witness." By dying, the martyr affirms that another person, a faith, a nation, or a value such as freedom or truth is worth the sacrifice of his or her own life; which is why tyrants, who have no problems about killing people, dislike making martyrs.

Albert Camus envisaged not merely death accepted passively in martyrdom but also death suffered when one goes down fighting, or even death inflicted in a just cause, as an affirmation, a *témoinage,* even a protestation of love. This affirmation, he insisted, is addressed, not only to the meek of the earth, but also and even more vehemently to oppressors and aggressors. There are times, he argued, when the only honest and fraternal attitude one can adopt toward another person is to oppose that person—even to the death.[1]

There are other situations in which death can be an affirmation. In *A Tale of Two Cities,* Sydney Carton sacrifices his own nondescript life to save Charles Darnay from the guillotine and reunite him with his wife and child. This affirmation of the life of a young family becomes, paradoxically, the redemption of his own life as well. In dying, Carton has at last managed to live. "It is a far, far better thing that I do, than I have ever done."[2]

A person may indeed lay down his or her life for somebody else, who is perceived as more precious, more worthy, or simply more vulnerable than oneself—often this will be a child. But it also happens that a person will die for a total stranger whose merits, if any, are simply unknown. Such self-sacrifice is not uncommon among lifeguards, firefighters, members of the security forces, or even casual passersby, who will risk life and limb to save an anonymous person, who, paradoxically, may even be engaged in attempting suicide.

The most extreme form of affirmation through death is to die for one's enemies. "While we were enemies we were reconciled to God by the death of his Son" (Rom 5:10). It has been suggested that Saint Paul's first intuition about Christ's death as love-sacrifice may have been born as he watched the death of Stephen, who, like Jesus, died praying for his killers (Acts 7:60).

Worth Living For/Worth Dying For

In adolescence, most of us probably dreamed of lives wagered for great causes or fair maidens, our regret being to have but one life so to squander. There were fantasies, too, and wonderful dreams, about that magical try, that goal, that vital home run, that snatched glory from the jaws of defeat at the very last moment. The reference to death in such wish-fulfilment fantasies is transparent. It betokens a deep desire to find meaning and worth in death as in life. There will be a final whistle. How shall I experience those closing moments, how shall I live them—in celebration, in hope, or in despair?

The alarming increase in suicides, especially among young males, is surely related to widespread poisoning of the imagination and of the capacity to create a hopeful future, even if only in the imagination. Substance abuse, hyperstimulation of the senses, uninhibited solicitations to toxic fantasies and dehumanizing behavior: all tend to pollute the wellsprings of imagination, leaving young people maimed in an essential faculty and less able to vision the future with courage and hope.

The tragedy is that when one has nothing worth dying for, one has nothing worth living for either.

Evading the Unavoidable

For many philosophies, death is not the affirmation of anything: it is simply the last word, the ultimate absurdity. In that perspective it seems better to ignore death and to enjoy one's brief spasm of existence. "Being unable to cure death, wretchedness, and ignorance, men have decided, in order to be happy, not to think about such things."[3] Instead, in Pascal's day as much as in our own, men busied themselves with sport, warfare, politics, lawsuits, hunting, or just about anything that would divert them from ultimate realities. Daudet's picture of the little goat nibbling grass while waiting for the wolf to devour her might be even more apposite in our own time.[4]

Can there be any in-depth human or spiritual growth, or even much excitement, in such a dumbed-down version of life?[5] Yet enormous amounts of time, money, and energy are expended on distracting ourselves from the real facts of life and death. The price we pay for this selective engagement with reality is a greater or lesser degree of neurosis, expressing itself in various unpleasant symptoms, of which unremitting and largely unfocused anxiety is probably the most characteristic. A concomitant result in our own day is a proliferation of exotic therapies and spiritualities offering to do the impossible: to square the psychological and spiritual short-circuiting within the human heart, without addressing the underlying problems of self-deception and elected immaturity.

Is it not odd to hear scornful denunciations of those, usually religious people, perceived as ignoring or repressing *eros*, while no one has a bad word to say about the tacit agreement to ignore death, repressing *thanatos*—right up to the moment when it suppresses us?

Death Is Natural but Never Banal

Death is usually sad. It may even be tragic, sometimes overwhelmingly so. Yet death is hardly evil; indeed it is natural. The truth is that, no matter what food we eat or abstain from, irrespective of what exercise we take, or which elixir of life we swear by, physically, chemically, biologically, and mechanically, we are not built to last. Some day we are going to wear out, expire, and return to the good earth from which we came. This is a wholesome, ecological, and wholly natural state of affairs.

Saint Francis speaks of Sister Death matter-of-factly, without surprise or morbidity. Saint Benedict invites his followers to keep death daily before (their) eyes, and to yearn for eternal life with all spiritual longing (RB 4:46–47). There is nothing life-hating about these attitudes; on the contrary, Benedict, like Francis, recognizes death as an integral part of our life story. They are looking at the total picture.

Nostalgia of the Heroes

One can understand the nostalgia of a postrevolutionary generation for the sacrificial death of martyred heroes, as expressed, for instance, by the Irish poet Máire Mac an tSaoi:

> Friends, when we die, it shall be in our beds,
> And having found no purchase worth the price,
> We'll part from life perforce and grudgingly,
> For us no trumpet and no sacrifice.[6]

Normal death is disappointing for such brave souls: it is the most routine and predictable of all human events. But, in sober truth, if opportunities for martyrdom or for dramatically sacrificial death do not arise in the experience of most people, it is probably just as well. The increasing numbers of suicide bombings and of other forms of self-immolation around the world show both the seductiveness and the ambivalence of that model.

The Death of Christ:
Paragon and Paradigm

Jesus spoke of his death as his great hour, when the Father's name would be glorified and he himself would be glorified by the Father (John 12:23,28; 17:1). This is the time when the Son will be lifted up and will draw all people to himself (John 12:32). Above all, it is the moment when he will pass from this world to the Father (John 13:1).

The essential gospel *kerygma,* as preached by the first disciples and as recorded by the evangelists, is centered on the death and glorification of Christ. Paul, for his part, scarcely speaks of anything else. His understanding of Christ, as of his own mission, and of the entire Christian life is rooted in that paschal mystery of life through death. The very logic of the incarnation requires that what is most central in the human experience of Christ will be at the very heart of our own.

It does not help that the traditional metaphors used to explicate the death of Christ—atonement, sacrifice, and redemption—are virtually void of meaning for our contemporaries. These concepts have little recognizable content for anybody except erudite scholars who are able to recreate the sociological and theological contexts in which they once had meaning. For ordinary people they ring hollow, when they do not actually mislead.[7] Simple evidence of this is the fact that nobody accompanying a dying person or the family of such a person nowadays would make prominent use of any of those images. What can we put in their place that will help us to enter on the mystery of Christ's death—and of our own?

We recognize that death can never be salvific, redemptive, or creative, merely as the brute spilling of sacrificial blood, nor as the material payment of a debt or penalty incurred by sins, nor yet as an atonement understood in purely juridical terms. We do try nowadays to place more emphasis on God's love and on the love of Jesus Christ. Even then we must be careful that negative or ambiguous notions about suffering and death as expressions of love do not lead us into something even worse.

If, when talking about the cross of Christ, we must indeed put the emphasis on love, we must not go on to imply that more pain means more love, and that, therefore, the death of Jesus was as ghastly as the Father could make it. This is barbaric thinking, and simply not true. The sufferings and death of Jesus on the cross were neither a sado-masochistic "ratcheting up" of love nor a lurid pedagogical exercise imposed by the Father on the Son just to make us all feel more guilty and ashamed of ourselves. This sort of presentation is dangerously akin to the sort of emotional blackmail that so thoroughly poisons relationships between parents and children and between lovers: "See how much I am suffering—and be miserable!" This will not help us to love God more or to humanize and live our own death in the way that Christ lived his. The meaning of the cross does not reside in the levels of awfulness achieved by the barbaric rituals of crucifixion.[8]

The death of Christ is *kenosis*, an emptying out of himself in perfect love for the Father and for us. This is the perfection and completion of that *kenosis* that is the incarnation, the self-emptying of God's own Self. In dying, Jesus went to the limit of what it means to be human. Having lived our life down to the last drop of his blood, he died our death. Completing the work of the incarnation in this way, the Son of God became fully man and opened the door for us, both to become fully human ourselves and to share in his divine life.

The point of contact between Jesus and ourselves is that we live short, fragile lives, beset by temptations and dangers, hemmed in by inadequacies and marred to a greater or lesser extent by our selfishness and sinfulness. We live in a world where people, out of stupidity, greed, lust, ambition, or sheer badness, inflict enormous cruelty and injustice on each other. It is precisely here that the Son of God has come to join and be with us.

Our Death

It is not a question of working out some theory about death that we will then try to assume existentially as we approach our last moments; still less, of preparing a suitably impressive last act for our personal drama. It is pointless to do so. For better or for worse, our dying will probably be the most authentic and personal thing we shall ever do: personal, in the sense that, sooner or later, we alone must do it—there being no possibility of substitute or alibi—and authentic, because here pretense and make-believe fall away, leaving at the end only the person whom we have become and who we are. In this sense, we shall all die as we have lived.

Mortality is not about a terminal moment—a moment when, in any case, many of us will not be conscious or in a position to inject any particular meaning into what is happening. Mortality is a common denominator of every aspect of human life. The challenge is not so much to know how to end life in good dispositions, but to learn how to live life fully, aware and accepting that we are fragile and mortal. This is what Saint Benedict has in mind when he tells us to keep death daily before our eyes. He is not being morbid: he is pointing us toward integrity and urging us to seek integration of all the aspects of our being.

Death Observed

Death is the consummation of whatever process of conversion and maturing a person has undergone throughout life. It is the process that is meaningful, rather than the event, whether or not that event is expected or sudden, violent or serene. What is important is to grow daily toward that maturity or, to express the same idea in Christian terms, to grow up to the full measure of Christ. As each person is unique, so will each be uniquely himself or herself in achieving that integration and entering upon that fullness of life.

Every family has its own sad and wonderful stories to tell about the death of a loved one, whether that death has been long awaited or has struck like a bolt from the blue. Such stories may seem anecdotal and trivial to outsiders; and to cynics, the merest wish fulfilment. Yet those who truly love are not mistaken in those moments when there is no dissimulation and nothing is superficial.

It is a solemn and deeply moving experience to accompany somebody in their last days.[9] It can also be extraordinarily liberating and enriching, both for the dying and for those who walk with them. There is liberation from fear and from a thousand anxieties, and enrichment in the discovery of unexpected peace and strength. Most surprising and delightful is a newfound capacity to express and to accept love in simplicity and joy.

It is, moreover, often the dying person, even somebody very young, who is seen to be strong and who prepares us for death, much more than we prepare them. Their serenity, discernment, and sureness of touch with each of many different persons surrounding them can be vastly impressive and reassuring. We are witnessing what is clearly a fruition of what is deepest and best in the dying person. It is a precious gift to have heard families speak so movingly of such experiences:

> "Those last weeks were the most beautiful, the happiest times we ever had together."
> "It was the best Christmas we ever had."
> "For the first time ever, we really talked to each other."
> "No inhibitions, no wondering what to do or say, no acting the part: we just cried and laughed together. It was so spontaneous and natural."

Here is a passage taken from a recent newspaper obituary that expresses beautifully an experience that many will have had.

> His sense of spiritual adventure grew as the end drew closer. It is a strange irony that many of us only learn to live life fully when death is imminent. He and his wife lived these last months with a joy and intensity that few, except the most enlightened, attain other than in the hour of crisis.
> His final moments were suffused with a sense of happiness, as he brought his family and loved ones with him to the edge of the abyss, made sure that they were serene and reconciled, and then bade farewell before he departed gently and in peace.[10]

This is the slow-release miracle close to its full flowering.

The Paschal Mystery

To die is not merely to fall asleep: it is to return to that point zero from which we emerged so mysteriously when first we began to be. It is to know the utter contingency of our own selves and of every created thing. At our original accession into life, we had neither the choice nor the possibility of knowing and accepting ourselves as the utter gift of God's creative love. In death, by contrast, after the slow pedagogy of life's experiences, as we are brought back to the threshold of existence, to the total poverty of our beginnings, we can at last know and accept ourselves fully for who we truly are.

Because who are we? Not just in this terminal moment, but in our lifelong experience of life itself and of death in life, who or what have we come to know ourselves to be? As all creation falls away from us, as our own faculties fail us, one by one, we know that, of ourselves alone, we are nothing. We did not create ourselves, nor can we maintain ourselves in being in any radical sense. "Can any of you by worrying add a single hour to your span of life?" (Matt 6:27). These facts become for us in the process of dying existentially certain and inescapable. It is only in the awareness of this utter poverty that we can grasp the extraordinary wonder of our being and know ourselves as pure gift of God's creative love, called out of nothingness to live not merely this transitory life, but to live and to love forever.

All true love says to the beloved, "You will never die." If, in saying this, human love promises more than it can deliver, yet it does not lie, because it is underwritten by God, who is love and the source of all love and life (1 John 4:7–8).

None of us has died, but all of us have come some way along that path. We have done some of our dying, and we may have been privileged to accompany another or others as they made that final journey. These may have been for us some of the most beautiful and reassuring experiences of our whole life. We have been learning the truth of this word of life: "Love has been perfected among us in this: that we may have boldness on the day of judgment, because as he is, so are we in this world. There is no fear in love, but perfect love casts out fear" (1 John 4:17–18). Beyond the ken of our own subjective experiences, let us look with faith and hope to what the Spirit is saying to our spirit in and through Jesus Christ, because even in this world we have become as he is. "For you have died, and your life is hidden with Christ in God. When Christ who is your life is revealed, then you also will be revealed with him in glory" (Col 3:3–4).

Christ, Son of God, is central and essential to our experience of death and resurrection because the moment in which we know ourselves as pure gift of love is the moment in which we discover our filiation. The immensity of God's gift and the inner mystery of our being is not just that, by God's creative act, we began to exist at some point in time as autonomous beings and will continue to subsist until, at some future moment, God withdraws that franchise again. We are not mere inventions, however wonderful. The secret of our being, the marvel, is that we are alive as sons and daughters in the Son. This means that the love of the Father for the Son is the bedrock, and the love of the Son for the Father is the dynamism, of our whole existence in time and in eternity.

The Son is born of the Father before time began: He is immortal. He is eternally Son of the Father. The man Jesus Christ is created within time. He is mortal and he will die. The last great cry of the dying Jesus is the ultimate self-expression of the Son in human form, of the Son-made-man: "Then Jesus, crying with a loud voice, said, 'Father, into your hands I commend my spirit.' Having said this, he breathed his last" (Luke 23:46). It is the inner life of the Trinity that is revealed in this moment of greatest human weakness, when the unshakable trust and love of the Son for his Father soars above every created thing and reaches out to that Father from whom he takes his being both in time and in eternity. Jesus dies and is glorified. Small wonder that the centurion should exclaim, "Truly this man was God's Son" (Mark 15:39).

The cry of Jesus, "Abba, Father!" is unceasing from the Garden of Gethsemane, where he prays that the chalice of suffering might pass him by (Matt 26:39ff), to his final commendation of himself to the Father in unwavering trust and love. This was, incarnated in our mortal flesh, the eternal response of the Son to the Father, who calls out to his Son, that day, as from all eternity, "You are my Son, today I have begotten you" (Ps 2:7; Heb 1:5).

Through the mystery of the incarnation, the Son of God lives out the mystery of his divine Sonship right down to the last drop of his blood; he dies and is glorified in the name of all humanity. The enormous significance of the cross and resurrection for us all is spelled out in the words spoken by Jesus to the dying thief: "Truly I tell you, today you will be with me in paradise" (Luke 23:43). No further words are needed to explain how this enfolding of our sinful humanity into the eternal love-dialogue of Father and Son in the Spirit is the perfect atonement for all sins, the undoing of all our failures in love and trust. As Saint Paul so truly says, "Where sin increased, grace abounded all the more" (Rom 5:20).

Saint Paul repeats in numerous ways the paradox of Christ's life-in-death at work within us. "We are always carrying in the body the death of Jesus, so that the life of Jesus may also be made visible in our bodies" (2 Cor 4:10). As we grow up to full maturity in Christ (Eph 4:13), we come "to know Christ and the power of his resurrection and the sharing of his sufferings by becoming like him in his death" (Phil 3:10). Paul is not talking here about physical ordeals followed by rewards: he is describing the whole process of transfiguration in Christ. "The Lord Jesus Christ will transform the body of our humiliation that it may be conformed to the body of his glory" (Phil 3:21). This is not just a physical change whereby the perishable puts on imperishability: it is the transfiguration whereby we, who have been modeled on the earthly man, will be modeled on the heavenly man, passing from the living soul of the first Adam to the life-giving spirit of Christ. This is the mystery, the secret hidden from the foundation of the world. Then the words of scripture will come true: Death is swallowed up in victory (1 Cor 15:43–58).

"We believe that Jesus died and rose again, even so, through Jesus, God will bring with him those who have died" (1 Thess 4:14). What does it mean to die *in* or *with* Jesus? Once again, it is not merely a matter of imitation, of going through the same physical ordeal. Nor is it some sort of juridical or moral identification whereby, as we undergo that ordeal, the good sentiments of Jesus are somehow attributed to us or substituted for our own real feelings. What is happening is something much more radical. We have become children of God in the Son who has shared our humanity (1 John 3:1). We have received his spirit. We have put on the mind of Christ (Phil 2:5).

> For all who are led by the Spirit of God are children of God. For you did not receive a spirit of slavery to fall back into fear, but you have received a spirit

of adoption. When we cry, "Abba! Father!" it is that very Spirit bearing witness with our spirit that we are children of God, then heirs, heirs of God and joint heirs with Christ—if, in fact, we suffer with him so that we may also be glorified with him. (Rom 8:14–17)

How wonderful, that the moment of our greatest weakness and the condition of our most utter poverty should be the time and the condition of our noblest and most meaningful act, the recognition and the joyful acceptance of the gift of God in Jesus Christ (John 4:10).

So let us thank God for giving us the victory through our Lord Jesus Christ (1 Cor 15:57).

CHAPTER FOURTEEN

Giving Thanks

Dostoevsky has defined man as "the ungrateful biped," which means ingratitude on two legs. We certainly do tend to know more about what else we want than about what we have already received. And we do take so very much for granted. Paradoxically, being ungrateful also springs from really low expectations. "Thanks for nothing!" Something I noticed in Moscow before the fall of Communism: in the shops, nobody said, "Thank you."

Some People

I once knew an old monk in a monastery far away who had been sent to a foundation of his European abbey in the pious hope that he would find something useful to do, something he was good at, something to afford him a little sense of fulfilment and achievement in life. He had not found any of this in his monastery of origin and, in the event, he was not to find it in his new monastic home either. The fact is that he was not really good at anything, and during a great number of years—because he lived to be a very old man—he was, in human terms, comprehensively useless and achieved nothing. His saving grace, from the community's point of view, was that he was no trouble: his needs were few, he was not demanding, and he did not get in the way of those dynamic confreres who tend to abound in young foundations.

I came upon this old man one day sitting in the monastery garden. This was just months before he died. "What do you do all day now, Father?" I asked—not maliciously, I hope, because the factual answer to my question would surely have had to be, "Nothing." I asked simply for the sake of saying something. He gave me a beautiful smile and said, "Oh, that is easy! I thank God; I just thank God all day." I did not ask incredulously, "For what?" because I realized at once in my heart that if only I could end my own days thanking God ceaselessly, my life would have been enormously worthwhile. Indeed, if I end my life any other way, what will it all have been about?

The wife of a prominent statesman and man of letters in my own country was involved in a horrendous road accident. For weeks, she hung in the balance between life and death. This man was an agnostic. Although grateful to the many people who were praying for his wife at this time, he could not bring himself to pray for her himself. It would have seemed to him as insincere and hypocritical.

One morning, when he arrived at the hospital to resume his daily vigil, he met the doctor on the stairway. This man seized him by the arm and said, "Good news, my friend: Your wife has turned the corner. She is going to live!" The husband himself recounts what happened next. Unable though he had been to pray, even to save his wife's life, he could not prevent himself in that moment from falling to his knees in heartfelt thanksgiving.

Good Sports

Many Irish people of my vintage still treasure a vivid iconic memory from the Melbourne Olympic Games of 1956. It is of Ronnie Delaney crossing the line to win gold for Ireland in the fifteen hundred meters. He falls to his knees, his arms raised above his head in a gesture of heartfelt thanksgiving.

Sportspeople do this sort of thing all the time. Their spontaneous instinct is to express exuberant celebration and even thanksgiving, not with the tip of their tongues, but with the whole splendid body that has just achieved a glorious triumph. I can call to mind numerous examples: from Stephen Roche winning the Tour de France in 1987, to a victorious jockey seen this very day on television blessing himself as he sailed past the post to win the Aintree Grand National.

Many will remember the famous goal and thanksgiving of Diego Maradona, who captained the Argentinean soccer team to glorious victory in the 1986 World Cup. A legendary goal indeed, and a fabulous thanksgiving, which have passed into history, with sporting good humor, as "The Hand of God."

Who knows whether God takes sides in sporting engagements—not to mention in wars or in politics? Whatever the case may be, the body language of sportspeople is always worth watching, in celebration, as in play. It is a language both expressive and truthful. Somersaults and punching the air do justice to routine achievements: truly unique moments call for something else and extra. Perhaps frustratingly for players themselves, awareness of the multimillion voyeurs watching their every move on television has made them coy about showing their deeper feelings.

Epiphany

Perhaps the most memorable of all the 317 covers that Norman Rockwell painted for the *Saturday Evening Post* between 1916 and 1963 was the one that showed a little old lady and a very small boy sitting at a table in a downmarket diner. Their heads are bowed, their hands clasped, as they say grace, thanking the good Lord for their less-than-gourmet repast. They are wholly absorbed, and unaware of the impression they are making on two young working men who share their table and on an older man standing nearby. Rough guys, all three of these, their faces are a study in quiet amazement, shocked reverence, and, in the case of the older man, one feels, a long forgotten tenderness. Sentimental? Yes, that would be our first line of defense against this powerful picture. It is like how Caravaggio might have painted the angels and the shepherds in a nativity scene.

Love

And what of love? There is an inspired scene in Zeffirelli's film version of *Romeo and Juliet*. Romeo, ecstatic, is scampering from the church where Juliet's Nurse has told him that her lady will come secretly that very day to Friar Lawrence's cell to meet and to marry him. Having run the length of the nave, the boy is about to hurtle through the door, when he wheels suddenly around to face the great crucifix suspended on the rood screen before the altar. Lifting both hands to his lips, he blows an enormous kiss to the Savior.

To love is indeed to be boundlessly grateful, not for this and that, so many quantifiable favors, but for the beloved, for the wonder of that person, and for the incredible gift of their love. If there is a hell, it must be a state of radical and irreversible ingratitude, a total incapacity to know oneself as uniquely loved and blessed. Francis Stuart the writer said in old age that what is even more important than to be loved is to be able to love. One cannot love if one has lost the plot of gratitude.

The Eucharist

The very essence of prayer is thanksgiving.[1] This is more important than all those mock-heroic oblations, all those sonorous and sometimes preposterous protestations of nothingness, those self-denigrating and inculpatory declamations, all those anxious, worried little invocations. Prayer, whether liturgical or personal, must focus primarily on what God is, and only incidentally on what man is not. The secret of prayer is to put God in the central position, to adore him, to delight in his beauty and goodness, to thank him with all our hearts, and to trust him for whatever is yet to come.

The Eucharist is the great prayer to the Father, of the only Son and inseparably of the church, which is his body. The heart and essence of this prayer is thanksgiving. The very word *eucharist* means to give thanks. "The Lord Jesus on the night when he was betrayed took a loaf of bread, and when he had given thanks, he broke it and said, 'This is my body that is for you. Do this in remembrance of me'"(1 Cor 11:23–24).

We acclaim every reading from the Word of God in the eucharistic liturgy with one or other of two responses: *Thanks be to God*, or *Praise to you, Lord Jesus Christ*. This shows plainly that praise and thanksgivings are not marginal extras: they are the church's unvarying response to everything that God is and does, to every word he has spoken, to every aspect of his revelation.

The various prefaces that introduce the eucharistic prayer, and the unvarying dialogue that sets the scene for the preface itself, leave us in no doubt about the emphasis and intent of what is to follow:

> The Lord be with you.
> And also with you.
>
> Lift up your hearts.
> We lift them up to the Lord.
>
> Let us give thanks to the Lord our God.
> It is right to give him thanks and praise.

This amounts not just to a statement of intent, but to a unanimous agreement of the whole assembly about why they have come together and what is to follow. The celebrant continues, "Father, all powerful and ever-living God, we do well always and everywhere to give you thanks and praise through Jesus Christ our Lord...."

Depending on the particular feast, season, or occasion, the preface goes on to recite particular motives for the church's unchanging sentiments of thanksgiving and joy. Whatever the circumstances, even in times of bereavement or tragedy, the central thrust of this keynote prayer is always the same: gratitude and trust. This is not to the exclusion of other sentiments—petition, oblation, grief, contrition— but if these are to be authentically Christian, and not merely human reactions of fear, guilt, or importunity in the face of some anonymous deity or force, they must stem from the specifically Christian recognition of God as Father.

Whatever our prayer, the radical starting point is always the awareness that we have received everything as pure gift. The first correlative of grace is gratitude.

The Prayer of Christ in His Church

In all of this, the prayer of Christ in his church is the vital basis and pattern for our personal prayer. *Sacramentum et exemplum,* the Latin fathers liked to say, meaning that Christ is both the model and the dynamic force behind what we do, whether as individuals or together as church. The joys and sorrows of individuals or of particular communities, their sufferings and their triumphs—all of this must be seen, not as so many isolated incidents or situations, but as a participation in Christ's paschal mystery of death and resurrection, as part of the working out of God's plan of salvation, as harbingers of the coming of his kingdom.

The coming of the kingdom must not be reduced to a random succession of good turns. We need the pedagogy and the reality, not just of public worship, but of *ecclesial* worship to make us understand that, above and beyond the particular favors that we may want to thank God for, we are joining with Christ and his body, the whole church, in thanking God for all that he is and for his total work of creation and recreation.

The seventy returned with joy, saying, "Lord, in your name even the demons submit to us!" This was thanksgiving of a sort, and for a notable favor. But Jesus wants his disciples to realize what God is offering, to recognize the Gift within the gift (John 4:10). "Do not rejoice at this, that the spirits submit to you, but rejoice that your names are written in heaven" (Luke 10:17–20). Even a prayer of thanksgiving can become a focus for individualism, elitism, and arrogance, a pretext to reject the common herd of God's people as crass, supine, and inept. "I thank you God that I am not like other people." The parable of the Pharisee and the publican (Luke 18:9–14) is a permanent reminder and a warning against prayer that is self-centered and fundamentally ungrateful.

CHAPTER FIFTEEN

Hope

> May the God of hope fill you with all joy and peace in believing, so that you may abound in hope by the power of the Holy Spirit. (Rom 15:13)

To believe in God, the God of hope, to allow him to be God; to believe in Jesus Christ, the one whom he has sent: this is the basis of our hope, our peace, and our joy. We must grow into this mystery, rather than circle endlessly around our own trite certainties. "O the depth of the riches and wisdom and knowledge of God! Who has known the mind of the Lord?!" Saint Paul exclaims (Rom 11:33–34). But he also makes bold to claim that we have the mind of Christ because we have received the gift of the Spirit, who alone knows the depths of God, and we are taught by the Spirit (1 Cor 2:11–16).

Paul constantly prays for our growth in knowledge, so that, "with the eyes of our hearts enlightened," we can see what hope God's call holds for us (Eph 1:18). That hope is centered on the unsearchable riches of Christ...the mystery hidden for ages in God...the eternal purpose that he has carried out in Christ Jesus our Lord, through whom we have access to God in complete confidence (Eph 3:8–11). He continues to pray that, rooted and grounded in love, we may have power to comprehend the breadth and length, the height and depth, and to know the love of Christ that surpasses knowledge, that you may be filled with all the fullness of God (Eph 3:17–19).

Paul likes to remind us that, during this life, we have hope but not vision to guide us (Rom 8:24–25). Saint John writes, "We are God's children now. What we will be has not yet been revealed. What we do know is this: when he is revealed, we will be like him for we will see him as he is. And all who have this hope in him purify themselves, just as he is pure" (1 John 3:2). The last sentence makes it clear that, though our ultimate destiny, and even our identity, are shrouded in mystery, this is no impediment to dynamic and meaningful action.

Abbot Denis Huerre remarks that we are, in this life, uncomfortably situated between the unconscious and the unknown. "Our desires come to us, at the surface, from this cave that we can never enter (the unconscious), but they are directed away from the cave toward something in the opposite direction that is equally mysterious. Their source is the subconscious that we can't know and their object is that which we don't yet know."[1] The unconscious is impenetrable and God is unknowable.

Yet hope is a powerful dynamo for action. "The monk," Huerre writes, "is one who desires and who desires to always go on desiring."[2] This is not the Camusian ideal of striving to *faire vivre l'absurde*. Not to know the meaning of my life does not mean that I am living an absurdity. It could mean instead that I am living at the heart of a mystery that I can only slowly and gradually begin to understand. Meaningful action becomes possible, less on the basis of problem solving and project management founded on solid information, and much more in terms of sensitivity in relationships, listening, and obedience to the voice of the Spirit. "Meaningful action is possible only against a horizon of expectation."[3]

> Uphold me, Lord, according to your word, and I
>   shall live,
> and do not disappoint me in my great expectations.[4]

Hope centered on God and on the person of Jesus Christ creates that horizon of expectation; ambition focused on limited objectives does not. Our call is to follow the Spirit, not to dream up and create a meaning for our own lives—if only because, in that self-centered perspective, we would always settle for too little. Glory to him, Paul exclaims, "whose power at work within us is able to accomplish abundantly far more than all we can ask or imagine" (Eph 3:20). "What no eye has seen, nor ear heard, nor the human heart conceived, what God has prepared for those who love him" (1 Cor 2:9). Such texts are not about greater material rewards than we could possibly imagine. They invite us instead to travel hopefully into the mystery of who we are destined to become in the project of God's creative love.

"To everyone who conquers I will give some of the hidden manna, and I will give a white stone, and on the white stone is written a new name that no one knows except the one who receives it" (Rev 2:17). The new name that is given to the victorious, and that is known only to the person who receives it, is the revelation to that person of who he or she really is, of what his or her life has been all about, and of each one's unique place in God's wonderful work of creation and salvation.

Know thyself! was the fundamental precept of ancient wisdom. If we are ever to achieve that fulfilment, we must allow God to be God. Made in God's own image (Gen 1:27), we can never know ourselves until we see and know ourselves in God. The secret of who we are and of what we are to become is inseparable from the mystery of God himself. Most of us, and I believe *all* of us, live and die without knowing our own beauty and the unique significance of our lives. The joy of heaven will be to see ourselves, at last, in the heart of God's love.

A Biblical Paradigm

We can take David as a biblical role model. He is not perfect, but there are so many attractive things about him: his loyalty to Saul, his love for Jonathan, his grief on account of Absolam, his courage, the sincerity of his repentance, the sheer enthusiasm of his dance.

Physical descriptions are rare in scripture. We have, for instance, no physical description of Jesus in the entire New Testament. Surprisingly, we do have a description of David as a teenager. In fact, it is given twice in almost the same words: "A lad of fair complexion, with fine eyes and a pleasant bearing." We are reminded, just before this description appears for the first time (1 Sam 16:12), that God does not see as human beings see; they look at appearances, but the Lord looks at the heart (1 Sam 16:7). We are probably to take this description, therefore, less as a celebration of physical beauty, and more as an evocation of David's demeanor, of what he is like in his heart, of how he responds, how he moves into the future, and, very specifically, of how he arrives to two of the most climactic experiences of his entire life.

The first time we read this description, David has been summoned urgently and is arriving to a family assembly from which he had originally been excluded as too young and too insignificant. He does not know what lies in store for him, but God has looked at his heart. Within minutes he will be chosen and anointed as king of Israel. "The Lord said, 'Rise and anoint him; for this is the one.' Then Samuel took the horn of oil, and anointed him in the presence of his brothers; and the spirit of the Lord came mightily upon David from that day forward" (1 Sam 16:12–13).

On the second occasion, the reason for including the nice-boy description of David is clearer. He is arriving to do battle single-handed against Goliath, the Philistine champion. Saul has been very dubious about this encounter, precisely because of David's physical condition. "You are not able to go against this Philistine to fight with him, for you are just a boy, and he has been a warrior from his youth" (1 Sam 17:33). As for Goliath, when he sees David arriving—*only a lad, with fair complexion and pleasant bearing*—he is filled with contempt and fury. He is outraged that this stripling should come out against him without so much as armor or proper weapons, as if chasing a dog with sticks. He curses David by all his gods. But exactly! It is the respective strength of David's God and all the gods of the Philistines that is going to determine the outcome of this contest. David is not depending on his own physical strength but on the Lord, who delivered him from claw of lion and paw of bear, and who will save him from the clutches of this Philistine (1 Sam 17:37).

On both of these occasions the point of the physical description is to show how David *arrives*, how he moves into the future. As we would probably say in our contemporary culture, What is his body language saying in each of these two crucial encounters with destiny? What is the picture?

David is attractive, but his attractiveness is more than skin deep.[5] It is the epiphany of his soul. We see him as confident but not arrogant. He is simple, bright, eager, naïve perhaps—with his Tom Sawyer catapult. We might call him *jaunty*. I suspect he may even have been whistling softly between his teeth: boys do that, you know, when they need to keep their courage up.

But David is not just Jack the Giant Killer. He is a man of destiny, open to the future and to whatever the Lord is doing through him. He is trusting, optimistic, full of hope. He is one who strides into the future with total confidence in God. The biblical evocation of his arrival is both charming and powerful. He is only a boy, but already his momentum comes from the inner voice that calls him into the future, his future and God's future. He is joyful in hope (Rom 12:12).

David puts me in mind of another of those wonderful, if politically ambiguous, slogans that I used to see on trucks in Nigeria: *One and God is majority!*

Hope's Horizon

The child, they say, is father of the man. David is the father of Jesus Christ, just as surely as Jesus is the son of David (Rom 1:3). This is the marvelous but hidden future toward which David steps out so jauntily. Christ is the deep meaning of David's incoherent hope, his mysterious horizon, the fulfilment toward which he steps out so cheerfully, with faith and trust. He knew in his heart that the news would be good: he lived and died without ever imagining just how good the good news of the gospel would be.

Christ is David's future. Christ is the future of all human nature. Christ is our future and our horizon. He is the fruit of the womb of our becoming. He is the Alpha, the beginning; he is also the Omega, the last, the end, and the goal. As the fulfilment and flowering of humanity, he is our meaning. The Desired One of all the nations, Jesus Christ is the son of Mary, and the son of David. He is also the son of each one of us. Saint Ambrose says it: "If according to the flesh, one woman is the mother of Christ, according to faith, Christ is the fruit of us all."[6]

Our faith is rooted in the past, in the saving events of salvation history, but it directs us into the future. A faith that looks only to the past in a spirit of conservation or restoration is faith without hope. David does not look back: he advances courageously, trusting in the future. As does Paul: "Forgetting what lies behind and straining forward to what lies ahead, I press on toward the goal for the prize of the heavenly call of God in Christ Jesus" (Phil 3:13–14). As does Jesus Christ, "who for the sake of the joy that lay in the future endured the cross, disregarding its shame" (Heb 12:2). Letting God be God means always being open to the new things that God is doing.

Our salvation is not in sight (Rom 8:24). But we know in whom we have believed. Whatever the difficulties—personal, communitarian, or ecclesial—let us step out together into the future with sublime jauntiness, assured that, through God's grace, our human nature, our David, is destined to grow, *will* grow up to the full measure of Jesus Christ.

"So, my dear brothers and sisters, be steadfast, immovable, always excelling in the work of the Lord, because you know that in the Lord your labor is not in vain" (1 Cor 15:58).

Epilogue

Then They Remembered His Words

"Why do you look for the living among the dead? He is not here, but he has risen. Remember how he told you, while he was still in Galilee, that the Son of Man must be handed over to sinners, and be crucified, and on the third day rise again." Then they remembered his words. (Luke 24:5–8)

We need to remember the words of the Lord Jesus, and to think about them. They are for us light and hope, most especially in times of darkness and sadness. Then the Word of God can speak to us in an intensely personal way. It is as if these words have been spoken and written down especially for us.

Let us remember the words of our Savior.

"I am the Resurrection and the life. Those who believe in me, even though they die, will live, and everyone who lives and believes in me will never die." (John 11:25–26)

"Do not let your hearts be troubled. Believe in God, believe also in me. In my Father's house there are

---

many dwelling-places. If it were not so, would I have told you that I go to prepare a place for you? And if I go and prepare a place for you, I will come again and take you to myself, so that where I am, there you may be also."(John 14:1–3)

"You have pain now; but I will see you again, and your hearts will rejoice, and no one will take your joy from you."(John 16:22)

"Truly I tell you, today you will be with me in Paradise." (Luke 23:43)

These are the words of the Lord. Their meaning is clear and unmistakable. Founded on the paschal mystery, on the death and resurrection of Christ, which we commemorate and celebrate in every mass, these words bring us to the heart of our Christian faith and hope.

What do we hope for? Saint Paul exclaims, "If for this life only we have hoped in Christ, we are of all people most to be pitied. But in fact Christ has been raised from the dead, the first fruits of those who have died" (1 Cor 15:19–20).

And it is Paul, too, who wrote, "I am convinced that neither death, nor life, nor angels, nor rulers, nor things present, nor things to come, nor powers, nor height, nor depth, nor anything else in all creation, will be able to separate us from the love of God in Christ Jesus our Lord" (Rom 8:38–39).

"God is love," Saint John tells us, "and those who abide in love abide in God, and God abides in them" (1 John 4:16).

My soul, and friend of my soul, you will never die!

Notes

Introduction

1. The initials "RB" refer to the Rule of Saint Benedict, and the abbreviation "Prol." refers to the prologue to that rule.

2. Tom Kettle, *The Day's Burden and Other Essays* (Dublin: Gill & Macmillan, 1968), 69.

CHAPTER ONE
What Must I Do?

1. Stendhal, *Scarlet and Black* (Baltimore: Penguin Classics, 1953), 195.

2. C. S. Lewis, "Hamlet: The Prince or the Poem," quoted from *Shakespeare's Tragedies: An Anthology of Modern Criticism*, ed. Laurence Lerner (London: Penguin, 1968), 79.

CHAPTER THREE
Who Is Jesus Christ?

1. Blaise Pascal, *Pensées* (Baltimore: Penguin Classics, 1966), 418.

CHAPTER FOUR
Approaches to the Mystery of Jesus

1. Hogwarts School is, of course, where Harry Potter and his friends, Ron and Hermione, are some of the *good wizard* students. Those who see the Harry Potter books as dark and dangerous may be reassured by John Killinger, *God, the Devil, and Harry Potter* (New York: St. Martin's Press, Thomas Dunne Books, 2002). I should declare an interest as an unabashed Harry fan myself.

2. Note that Jesus wrote *twice* with his finger on the stone floor of the Temple, just as Yahweh wrote twice in stone on Mount Sinai. See Andrew Nugent, OSB, "What Did Jesus Write?" *Downside Review* (July 1990): 193–98.

CHAPTER FIVE
Conversion: The Project

1. *The Sayings of the Desert Fathers,* trans. Benedicta Ward (Kalamazoo: Cistercian Publications, 1984), 204.

2. Evagrius, *Ad Monachos,* 107; *The Mind's Long Journey to the Holy Trinity,* trans. Jeremy Driscoll (Collegeville, MN: Liturgical Press, 1994).

3. Columba Stewart, OSB, in *Purity of Heart in Early Ascetic and Monastic Literature,* ed. H. Luckman and L. Kulzer (Collegeville, MN: Liturgical Press, 1999).

4. Evagrius, *Pratikos,* 6–14; Cassian, *Conferences 5,* and *Institutes 5–12.*

5. Simon Tugwell, OP, *Ways of Imperfection: An Exploration of Christian Spirituality* (Springfield, IL: Templegate, 1985), 27.

CHAPTER SIX
Conversion: The Grace

1. Mark returns so often and so robustly to the theme of the disciples' incomprehension that Matthew and Luke find it necessary to attenuate both the frequency and the vehemence of his allusions.

2. It is the philosophy of the Common Man in Robert Bolt's play, *A Man for All Seasons.*

CHAPTER SEVEN
A Lenten Life

1. Several passages in this chapter and in the next are copied from Andrew Nugent, OSB, "Benedict's Easter," *American Benedictine Review* (December 2003). I am grateful for the editor's permission.

CHAPTER EIGHT
A Church?

1. Kathleen Norris, *Amazing Grace: A Vocabulary of Faith* (New York: Riverhead Books, 1998), 78ff. This book is a splendid reintroduction to religion as inheritance.

2. Henri Bergson, *The Two Sources of Morality and Religion,* trans. A. Audra and C. Brereton (Notre Dame, IN: University of Notre Dame Press, 1977).

3. See Philip Jenkins, *The New Anti-Catholicism: The Last Acceptable Prejudice* (Oxford: Oxford University Press, 2003), and by the same author, *Pedophiles and Priests* (Oxford: Oxford University Press, 1996).

4. *The Life of St. Benedict,* ed. A. de Vogüé, trans. H. Costello and E. de Bhaldraithe (Petersham, MA: St. Bede's Publications, 1993). The *life* is traditionally attributed to Pope Saint Gregory the Great.

5. Denis Huerre, *Letters to My Brothers and Sisters: Living by the Rule of St. Benedict* (Collegeville, MN: Liturgical Press, 1994), 71.

6. The Greek word *ekklesia* was used to translate the Hebrew *kahal* in the Bible, meaning the assembly of all the people coming together. Transposed into Latin as *ecclesia,* this word is the basis for the word for *church* in nearly all modern European languages, for example, *église* in French. The essential idea of "church" is the bringing together of all God's people.

7. Fyodor Dostoevsky, *The Brothers Karamazov,* vol. 1, trans. D. Magarshack (London: Penguin Classics, 1958), 339.

8. Anotoine de Saint-Exupéry, *Pilote de Guerre* (Paris: Gallimard, 1942), 213. (Translated as *Flight to Arras,* London: Penguin, 1961.)

9. *"Le moi n'est pas un étant 'capable' d'éxpier pour les autres: il est cette expiation originelle."* Emmanuel Levinas, *Autrement qu'être ou au delà de l'Essence* (The Hague: Martinus Nijhoff, 1974), 151.

10. Xavier Le Pichon, *Aux Racines de l'Homme: De la Mort à l'Amour* (Paris Presses de la Renaissance, 1997), 262.

CHAPTER NINE
One Man's Celibacy

1. Paul Evdokimov, *The Sacrament of Love* (New York: St. Vladimir Press, 1985).

2. Ibid., 156.

3. Richard Sipe, *Celibacy: A Way of Loving, Living, and Serving* (Liguori, MO: Liguori, 1996), 196.

4. Tomaš Špidlík, *The Spirituality of the Christian East* (Kalamazoo: Cistercian Publications, 1986), 162. It is regrettable that Chrysostom's rich theology of marriage is frequently ignored by Western writers, who look no further than his *de Virginitate,* an early work where Chrysostom adopts the artless ploy of praising celibacy by denigrating marriage. This is not representative of the man nor of his mature thought.

5. Much of what follows has already appeared in "One Man's Celibacy," *The Tablet* (January 14, 1995).

CHAPTER TEN
The Little Black Girl in Search of God

1. The title is borrowed from George Bernard Shaw; the substance appeared originally as an article in *Spirituality* (September–October 1997).

2. Carl Jung, *Memories, Dreams, Reflections* (London: Fontana , 1986), 276.

CHAPTER ELEVEN
Monastic Spirituality

1. This chapter is substantially copied from my contribution to *The Search for Spirituality: Seven Paths within the Catholic Tradition,* ed. Stephen Costello (Dublin: The Liffey Press, 2002). I am grateful to the editor and publisher, while acknowledging also the other essays in that book and the spiritual paths that they describe.

2. See, for instance, Kathleen Norris, *The Cloister Walk* (New York: Riverhead Press, 1996).

3. 1 Pet 4:11, quoted in RB 57:9.

4. See chapter 13 of this book, "Has Death a Meaning?".

CHAPTER TWELVE
Signs of the Seeker

1. For a fuller treatment, see Andrew Nugent, OSB, "Benedict: A Sense of Prayer," *American Benedictine Review* (June 1999): 149–60.

2. Guigo 11, *Scala Claustralium* 2. On the whole topic of *lectio*, see Michael Casey, *Sacred Reading: The Ancient Art of Lectio Divina* (Liguori, MO: Liguori, 1996).

3. Casey, *op. cit.*, Preface vi.

CHAPTER THIRTEEN
Has Death a Meaning?

1. Albert Camus, *L'Homme Révolté* (Paris: Gallimard, 1963), *passim*. Camus was a *pied-noir*, a French Algerian. His ideas, born at the cusp of two great civilizations, speak today in a situation where these civilizations seem increasingly to be in conflict. See Samuel Huntington, *The Clash of Civilizations and the Remaking of World Order* (New York: Simon & Schuster, 1996).

2. Charles Dickens, *A Tale of Two Cities* (London, Collins, 1962), 414.

3. Blaise Pascal, *Pensées* (Baltimore: Penguin Classics, 1966), 133.

4. Alphonse Daudet, *Lettres de Mon Moulin* (Paris: Nelson, 1943), 56.

5. Whatever about popular culture, serious philosophers have always tried to face up to the reality of death. See, for

an excellent summary, "Learning to Die," in Pierre Hadot, *Philosophy as a Way of Life* (Oxford, UK, and Cambridge, MA: Blackwell, 1995), 93ff.

6. From the poem "For Fergus," in Máire Cruise O'Brien, *The Same Age as the State* (Dublin: O'Brien Press, 2003), 142. The poet/author uses different versions of her name for different purposes.

7. Yann Martel's splendid novel *Life of Pi* sketches an amusing yet sharply on-target critique of such sclerosed catecheses of the paschal mystery, while at the same time suggesting the way to transcend it. Yann Martel, *Life of Pi* (Edinburgh: Canongate, 2002), Ch. 17.

8. I would have serious reservations, on these grounds, about Mel Gibson's film, *The Passion of the Christ*.

9. See Michael Kearney, *Mortally Wounded* (Dublin: Marino/Mercier, 1996).

10. Aengus Fanning, Obituary for Peter O'Brien, *Sunday Independent*, November 2, 2003.

CHAPTER FOURTEEN
Giving Thanks

1. See Andrew Nugent, OSB, "Masses in Thanksgiving," in *Making the Most of the Ritual Readings*, ed. Cathal O'Flanagan, OFM (Dublin: Dominican Publications, 1978), 193ff.

CHAPTER FIFTEEN
Hope

1. Denis Huerre, *Letters to My Brothers and Sisters: Living by the Rule of St. Benedict* (Collegeville, MN: Liturgical Press, 1994), 100.

2. Ibid. (i.e., also p. 100, as in note 1).

3. Jürgen Moltmann, *The Theology of Hope* (London: SCM, 1967), 327.

4. A conflation of Psalms 118 and 116, from Saint Benedict's ceremony of monastic profession (RB 58).

5. In purely physical terms, David's treacherous son, Absalom, was probably even more attractive than his handsome father (2 Sam 14:25–26).

6. Saint Ambrose, *Commentary on Luke's Gospel*, 2:26.